STUDIES IN ENGLISH LIT

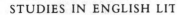

General Edito

David Daiches

Already published in the series:

Already published in the series (*continued*):

SHAKESPEARE:
ANTONY AND CLEOPATRA

by
ROBIN LEE

EDWARD ARNOLD

First Published 1971 by
Edward Arnold (Publishers) Ltd
41 Bedford Square, London WC1B 3DQ

Reprinted 1974, 1975, 1978, 1981 (twice)

ISBN: 0 7131 5588 4

For Anina

Printed and bound in Great Britain at
The Camelot Press Ltd, Southampton

General Preface

The object of this series is to provide studies of individual novels, plays and groups of poems and essays which are known to be widely read by students. The emphasis is on clarification and evaluation; biographical and historical facts, while they may be discussed when they throw light on particular elements in a writer's work, are generally subordinated to critical discussion. What kind of work is this? What exactly goes on here? How good is this work, and why? These are the questions that each writer will try to answer.

It should be emphasized that these studies are written on the assumption that the reader has already read carefully the work discussed. The objective is not to enable students to deliver opinions about works they have not read, nor is it to provide ready-made ideas to be applied to works that have been read. In one sense all critical interpretation can be regarded as foisting opinions on readers, but to accept this is to deny the advantages of any sort of critical discussion directed at students or indeed at anybody else. The aim of these studies is to provide what Coleridge called in another context 'aids to reflection' about the works discussed. The interpretations are offered as suggestive rather than as definitive, in the hope of stimulating the reader into developing further his own insights. This is after all the function of all critical discourse among sensible people.

Because of the interest which this kind of study has aroused, it has been decided to extend it first from merely English literature to include also some selected works of American literature and now further to include selected works in English by Commonwealth writers. The criterion will remain that the book studied is important in itself and is widely read by students.

DAVID DAICHES

Contents

1. The Nature of the Play

(i) Tragedy and tragic theory

The study of dramatic tragedy presents peculiar difficulties to the student of literature. Ironically, these difficulties arise because of the amount of theorising that has been done about drama since Aristotle categorised the different elements of tragedy. The efforts of critics to produce totally comprehensive theories of tragedy have not always clarified the plays. Indeed, they have often complicated, and in some cases quite distorted our view of tragic drama. In the first place, such theorising immediately sets up a tension between the theoretical standard and the play itself. All too often, then, the critic succumbs to the temptation to manipulate his response to the play rather than alter or dismantle his categories. Attachment to any one theory of tragedy can also lead to unfortunate results. Among these is the pointless wrangling about whether *Antony and Cleopatra* (or any other play) is or is not a tragedy. These arguments are carried on with a violence that suggests that they are not just conflicts over terms. Rather, critics will behave as if there were some ideal category of 'tragedy', the purity of which must be maintained by a policy of exclusion. The worst that can result here is that the critic becomes trapped in his own categories to the extent that he is no longer able to re-experience the play at all.

Generalising from one tragedy to others also has its dangers, though it avoids the worst excesses of theoretical discussion. For instance, among these dangers is the habit of assuming that all tragedies must contain a definite moral pattern simply because some tragedies do. If this moral pattern—or, even worse, moral statement—is not obvious (as it is not in *Antony and Cleopatra*), the critic may shift the dramatist's emphasis to make a moral drama out of it. Or he will proclaim that the play is not a tragedy. In the case of *Antony and Cleopatra*, starting with such assumptions will impel the critic to take one side or the other in the conflict between love and duty. In the case of *Hamlet*, this critical attitude calls on us to attribute to Hamlet a horror of killing a man for revenge that the text itself does not substantiate; for the moral critic is always impelled to attribute to the hero moral scruples similar to the critic's.

Any theory of tragedy that aims at coherence and exclusiveness is likely to have some of these failings, especially if suggestions of a superior *kind* of drama are associated with the term 'tragedy'. On the other hand, some flexible categories of tragedy are helpful, and must anyway be in the critic's mind once he has read more than one work with a tragic conclusion. A flexible attitude, aiming at seeing different kinds of tragic processes and different qualities of tragic effect, seems thus more helpful.

We need to be flexible in two ways. First, we need to see that certain critical emphases are more appropriate to one tragedy than another, and to use the more appropriate in elucidating any particular play. In *Antony and Cleopatra*, this will mean emphasising the mythic and ritualistic elements—present in, but not vital to, other tragedies—and stressing the full experience of the play rather than a moral resolution of the opposites presented. In *Macbeth*, conversely, the resolution of the conflict and the re-establishment of social and moral order are the important elements, along with the hero's inner awareness of his tragic conflict. As Arnold Stein writes:

> Antony is no explorer of consciousness. He has very little Hamlet or Macbeth in him.[1]

It would be unacceptably narrow to go on to suggest that, lacking such self-consciousness, Antony is not a tragic hero, and Mr. Stein does not. Antony's tragedy *is* the tragedy of the imaginative, public gesture of nobility defeated by the sordid public fact. The mythic suggestions in the play are also related to the public quality of his expression of character, as are the ritual processions and meetings. We see then that we cannot make much of Antony's tragedy from Macbeth's, nor of Macbeth's from Antony's. Yet both are experiences that we recognise as tragic.

The other flexibility required of us is in our view of drama itself, especially in its relation to our own concerns. Some plays are overtly didactic, and some do speak directly to us concerning our own lives or times—or at least, they contain issues that we can translate into those terms. Others, tragedy among them, bear a more distant, a symbolic relation to our lives; a relation, we might say, we can respond to but cannot use. Such plays are not important to us through any definite meaning we can give to them, nor through their help in our own lives. Rather, they are best seen as:

[1] 'The Image of Antony: lyric and tragic imagination', *Kenyon Review*, Vol. XXI, 1959, pp. 586–606

a non-discursive symbolic form . . . able to sustain a texture of contradictions, opposites, paradoxes and ambiguities and to communicate
them to an audience . . . that does not limit its response by intellectual-
ising it.[2]

(ii) *Our experience of drama*

If we approach tragedy in this way, we see that our experience of the
play is initially our experience of the action, of the sequence of events as
they occur on the stage. We will respond, obviously, to the tone and
force of speeches, but the way in which the characters *act* will be our first
deep experience. The critic's task should thus be to elucidate, not the
meaning, but rather the experience of the play; beginning with our
response to the action. Much recent criticism has emphasised this point,
and I think that this is more than a fashionable objection to the previous
fashion of emphasising imagery and verbal texture. It is a re-assertion of
the idea that the enactment is the source of the tragic effect, and that the
meaning arises from the total movement of the play. As all drama
centres on conflict, this movement will by its nature contain contradictory elements, and so also will the meaning of the play. The audience's
experience of the play will depend upon the quality and speed of the
action and the kind of resolution it is brought to, as well as upon the
tone of the speeches; upon the grouping and stances of the actors upon
the stage, as well as on the patterns of imagery.

In terms of this approach it follows also that the form of the play will
be conditioned by the dramatist's knowledge of the audience's expectations, and that analysing the form will be to show him controlling and
directing these expectations towards his required conclusions. Thus once
again our emphasis falls upon the dynamic quality of the dramatic
action.

In *Antony and Cleopatra* our experience of the action of the play is
of two kinds. Most obviously, there is the spectacle of 'greatness going
off', of the process of a tragic decline to defeat and death which is established as inevitable early in the play. Shakespeare also causes the tragic
figures to make their respective stands against this process—though he
always supplies a soothsayer (II, iii, 16), or an Enobarbus (II, vi, 116),
or even a common soldier (III, vii, 61) to remind us of the major

[2] S. A. Shapiro, 'The Varying Shore of the World: ambivalence in
Antony and Cleopatra', *Modern Language Quarterly*, Vol. XXVII, 1966,
pp. 18-32

movement. Yet through these stands, and especially in the quality of their love, defying the tragic movement, Antony and Cleopatra create another level of action. This level of action has been variously described as 'this sense of having a rôle of greatness to live up to' (Holloway) and 'imaginative gestures that project the self [Antony] has in his mind's eye' (Stein). What is implied is that, at moments, both Antony and Cleopatra assert, in speech and deed, a quality of life that strikes us as superior to the forces massed against it, but which is nevertheless going to be destroyed by those forces. They themselves also continually betray their finer qualities, as well as having them mocked by lesser men. Yet, at these crucial points, these qualities enter the audience's experience as part of the movement of the play. Such points would include Antony's first speech (I, i, 33), Cleopatra's parting words in a later scene (I, iii, 86), and Antony's 'Fall not a tear, . . .' (III, xi, 69), as well as Act IV, Scenes xiv and xv, and much of Act V. In each case, though much of the force of the assertion lies in the words, the moment is also one of action. Antony does not talk to the messengers, Cleopatra does let him go, Antony does forgive her her desertion. Our experience of the play must include both the tragic movement and these movements of spirit against it.

The nobility and greatness of the tragic characters is further reinforced by the mythic, even divine, status given them, and the hints of ritual to be felt in their imaginative gestures. It seems to me that it is this quality of ritual and formality, with glimpses of mythic situations and groupings, that helps to create the deep suggestive power of these scenes, and thus contribute to the final tragic effect. These ritual or mythic glimpses become part of our experience of the play because they are activated in us by word and action, though the degree to which they are taken up by the audience is again controlled by the dramatist. Many modern critics have emphasised the archetypal patterns of general human experience that lie beneath the immediate personal concerns of the tragic hero. In fact, it is almost generally agreed that certain ritual patterns do exist within, and give valuable extension to, all tragedies. These patterns can be seen in several ways. A scene itself may be openly organised along these lines, as in Lear's formal division of his kingdom, or in the disruption of the formal banquet in *Macbeth*. In both cases, deep divisions beneath a superficially harmonious state are enacted by the breaking down of an established order, and the loosening of ties of loyalty and obligation.

Or a mythic aspect may be hinted at in the grouping of figures and by verbal allusions, as Hamlet's outlaw status, partly forced upon him and partly accepted, is suggested by his stance apart from the courtiers, a black figure, fearing and feared. Or, again, a sense of mythic extension may be suggested in the poetry and negated in the action, as is Antony's status as Mars. In this last case a tension, leading to irony, is set up between the audience's expectations of power and freedom in the mythic figure, and his actual subordination to social forces and to the nature of things as they are.

In all these cases, the critic's task is to identify these ritual suggestions and mythic shapes, which will be *felt* by the audience. I am not here proposing some form of dramatic collective unconsciousness, but trying to emphasise that our response to the formal, detached portrayal of action that we find in tragedy, at least, is quite different from our response even to similar situations in life. The effect of tragedy as a dramatic form lies largely in those differences—its deeper suggestiveness, its power to move the audience, finally its paradoxical power to provide pleasure from the spectacle of a tragic death.

To identify and describe such aspects of the audience's experience of the play is a helpful approach to all tragedy. It is the most appropriate for *Antony and Cleopatra*. Its peculiar quality is that it is a dangerous and impossible play to pin down in a formulated meaning. This is the result of elements such as the insistence upon a dialectical movement, both in space and in moral value, the ambiguous status of the tragic characters and the emotional effect of the tragic deaths. Certainly any statement of 'meaning' would either be so full of qualifications, of 'buts' and 'yets', as to be quite unhelpful; or, lacking them, would do less than justice to the play. Here, if anywhere in Shakespeare, it is a case of the whole play being the thing, because no movement or judgement in the play is finally abandoned, no point of view entirely discredited. Octavius shows conflicting traits—duty and overwhelming ambition. Enobarbus is reasonable and disloyal, Pompey polite and treacherous, Antony stern and lascivious. None of these characters is finally accounted for according to some moral standard that emerges in the course of the play, in a way at all comparable to the sense of finality we feel about our judgements on Claudius, Iago, Goneril or Regan.

This is partly because the tragedy does not generate sufficiently clear-cut moral canons to settle our view of these characters. It is also because, in their movement through the play, they show their widely different qualities to us at different times. Of course, this duality of vision is clearest when we look at the two main characters. There, our sense of the futility of their deaths conflicts with our sense of the nobleness and value of the same acts. This conflict is not resolved in the play. We confront similar issues about several of the minor characters also, and this once again contributes to our sense that we will get more from our experience of the movement of the play than from identifying a 'meaning'. More of the importance of seeing the dynamic quality of the play will come out when we analyse the structure and the characters. But first two other points need to be made, concerning the mythic quality of the play, and the fact that moral issues are not dominant in our experience of it.

There is little doubt that this tragedy involving two all-too-human characters does still create a mythic dimension in our minds. There is no doubt that the other characters in the play feel that Antony and Cleopatra have semi-divine status. Philo, in a speech mostly critical of Antony, compares him (in the fourth line of the play) with Mars, and throughout the play he is associated with that god and with Hercules, by legend an ancestor of Antony's. For instance, Antony himself sees his tragic suffering in terms of the Hercules legend:

> The shirt of Nessus is upon me, teach me,
> Alcides, thou mine ancestor, thy rage.
> Let me lodge Lichas on the horns o' the moon,
> And with those hands that grasp'd the heaviest club,
> Subdue my worthiest self. (IV, xii, 43–7)

Cleopatra is consistently compared to both Venus, goddess of love, and Isis, the Egyptian goddess mythically associated with militant sexuality, fertility and maternity. Enobarbus' speech describing her progress down to Cydnus is the most sustained example, but others are to be found all over the play.

The transcendent power of their love is first suggested by Antony himself:

> Then must thou needs find out new heaven, new earth. (I, i, 17)

Cleopatra later echoes that quality:

> Eternity was in our lips, and eyes,
> Bliss in our brows' bent: none our parts so poor,
> But was a race of heaven. (I, iii, 35–7)

Much later in the play Antony sees the beginning of his defeat in similarly mythic terms:

> . . . our terrene moon
> Is now eclips'd, and it portends alone
> The fall of Antony! (III, xiii, 153-5)

As he is dying, he foresees a divine after-life for both of them:

> Dido, and her Aeneas, shall want troops,
> And all the haunt be ours. (IV, xiv, 53-4)

Even Caesar, who has previously called him 'an old ruffian', comments on Antony's death in similar terms:

> . . . The death of Antony
> Is not a single doom, in the name lay
> A moiety of the world. (V, i, 17-19)

Finally, as we shall see in greater detail later, Cleopatra's speeches about Antony after his death are full of references to his great, mythic stature. In these ways, the human love and the tragic destruction of two historical personages take on, in *our* imaginations as well as in their own, the dimensions of an archetypal human experience. In their story is presented the eternal conflict of personal satisfactions with impersonal duty, raised by the poetry to a high degree of power and splendour, and eventually becoming the paradigm, the myth, in which the essence of that particular human experience is embodied for us. This mythic quality was present in the story as Shakespeare received it, but he focuses upon it through the rhetoric of the poetry, and the ritual nature of several of the situations.

I will deal more fully with details of these scenes in later chapters, and intend here only to glance at the broad archetypal pattern that under-lines this, and other tragedies. Both Holloway and Frye regard this pattern as one of sacrifice. The tragic hero initially appears as the scape-goat or outlaw, a man who is partly cast out by, and partly repudiates, his society. His tragic fall, the sense of 'greatness going off' that is associated with him, consequently follows two courses. He is, in one way, destroyed by his society. He has repudiated it, and it repudiates him for violating its beliefs or practices. In another way, this process is also one in which, by coming to accept his position as outlaw, the hero discovers what is authentically himself, and thus gains self-knowledge and a large measure of sympathy from the audience. The audience's deepest cultural feelings are activated in response to the outlaw figure, who offers them a vision of a freedom beyond their own, combined with a warning about the consequences of claiming that freedom. Again it seems to me that this kind of analysis both illuminates all tragedy and in particular gives insight into *Antony and Cleopatra*, where we have already seen the dramatist's own insistence upon the general and the mythic qualities of the action. To point to such a pattern is not, of course, to provide a total interpretation, and anyone approaching the play will do well to keep in mind Frye's own insight into the ranges of interpretation possible:

> *Antony and Cleopatra* is . . . the story of the fall of a great leader [and thus tragic]. But it is easy to look at Mark Antony ironically as a man enslaved by passion; it is easy to recognise his common humanity with ourselves; it is easy to see him as a romantic adventurer of prodigious courage and endurance betrayed by a witch; there are even hints of a superhuman being whose legs bestrid the ocean and whose downfall is a conspiracy of fate, explicable only to a soothsayer. To leave out any of these would oversimplify *and belittle* the play.[3]

To draw this section together, then, we can see that the play contains a tension between two kinds of action. One of these movements is associated with the tragic decline, the other with resistance, with the gestures Antony and Cleopatra create against that decline. The second movement is given further substance by the mythic quality of the story and characters, and by the force of the poetry. Here we approach the core of the ambivalent effects so typical of the play. Every failure in action has set against it a magnificent gesture or speech; each such gesture is followed by another failure. Nowhere do the two meet, and in fact the audience are forced to contemplate an ever-widening dichotomy. One movement tends to degrade the figures, the other to deify them— and both are true.

(iii) *Totality of awareness*

It is this sort of complexity that makes it impossible to take *Antony and Cleopatra* as a moral drama. Yet, it has often been taken as one. Indeed, the history of critical discussion of the play is largely a history of changing fashions in proclaiming the love to be an acceptable ideal or, alternatively, a destructive passion. These responses probably arise from an assumption that, because the play incorporates moral acts and judgements and the critic is interested in moral value, the play itself must finally make a moral statement. Again, *Antony and Cleopatra* is something of a test case, because moral judgements abound in the play, and yet, as history shows, the moral import of the play itself is far from clear.

---

[3] *Anatomy of Criticism*, Princeton, 1957, p. 51

Once again, a shift of attention to the dynamic quality of the play, to the ambiguities and contradictions that are contained in the actual movement, helps us to escape this particular dead-end. If, using Holloway's terms again, we focus our attention on what is 'transacted' rather than on what finally 'transpires', then there appears a dramatic quality in the whole play which is quite different to the moral quality of any individual choice, or even the crucial tragic choice. The dramatic (and poetic) quality of the play is now seen to lodge in the *evocation* of the situation, and not in its *resolution*. Even if we accept, for the moment, that Antony's choice of love over duty is an 'immoral' choice, Shakespeare creates such interest in, and response to, the motives, feelings, fears and joys associated with that choice, that we are aware of an emotional response that does not depend on the morality of the choice at all. The weight of our involvement in what is transacted upon the stage is greater than our interest in the morality or immorality of Antony's choices, judged by any standard within or outside the play. W. K. Wimsatt has summed up this distinction between the moral and dramatic qualities of the play:

> Neither a wrong choice nor a right one . . . excludes the awareness of many values, some interrelated and supporting, some rival, some sacrificed by a choice, some in situations held in ironic balance or entering into unresolved tensions. Poetry, by its concreteness and dramatic presentation of value situations . . . by the very fulness and hence imaginative power of its presentation, has the meaning and being which makes it poetry. That *is* the poetic value.[4]

Antony and Cleopatra, as he shows, has this kind of power. So, to return to the central theme of this chapter, we see that the distinctive quality of this play consists of what Wimsatt calls 'concrete and dramatic presentation of value situations' and what I will call 'totality of awareness'. In other words, the forces and values created in the play might be used to show either a world well lost for love, or a man of power and responsibility destroyed by an illicit passion; but an audience's experience will actually cover both these alternatives, and more, since acknowledging both creates a tension that neither alternative alone evokes. Shakespeare creates, in the familiar story, a conflict of love and responsibility within Antony, and then by action, image and rhetoric, extends this conflict through the 'wide arch of the rang'd Empire'. Yet we cannot find the inner conflict more important than the outer.

[4] *The Verbal Icon*, University of Kentucky Press, 1967, p. 98

Similarly, neither of them dominates the other conflict between Caesar and Cleopatra. In Cleopatra, we feel the force of a changing, unpredictable, vital but potentially degrading concern with the self and the present. In Octavius, we feel the force of a stable, reliable, polite, but potentially degrading concern with the state and the future. Neither removes the other's force. At all these levels—the conflict within Antony, between Antony and his world, and between Cleopatra and Octavius— the final position reached is ambivalent. Antony dies, yet in a sense triumphs over himself in the quality of his death; he is defeated by circumstances, yet asserts an emotional value that circumstance cannot touch. Octavius is militarily triumphant, but must pay grudging homage to the quality of Cleopatra's death, to which we in turn give even greater value. At the same time, the play by no means negates the Roman values—witness how Stoic endurance is sought at the end by both Antony and Cleopatra—and indeed creates them with a peculiar force, as in the scenes involving Enobarbus and Eros in Act IV.

The position in which we find ourselves, then, is this: the total quality of a situation is evoked by the play, and no single force, action or judgement within the totality is entirely acceptable to Shakespeare, or can be seen as entirely correct by the audience. We feel ourselves called upon to respond more to the fulness of the situation than to make any judgement of the actions. Indeed, the partial and illusory nature of the characters' own assessments is no inducement to join them in the hopeless task of pinning down a changing and contradictory situation in a formulated judgement. Instead of judging, the audience is asked rather to see why a certain action is performed by a certain character in certain circumstances. In a less pointed way, something of this relative quality is found in all drama; but in *Antony and Cleopatra* the relative quality of all human judgements is not simply a dramatic fact, but one of the themes of the play, and an important element of the structure.

We see it as a theme most clearly in the life of Enobarbus. Early in the play, he is presented as something of a cynic, certainly a detached observer. He maintains that role in the early exchanges between Antony and Octavius. We first become aware of conflicts in our view of him when he is given the speech evoking Cleopatra's royal beauty. During Acts III and IV, he maintains the power of reason against Antony's passion, and, though aware of an internal conflict, eventually makes a rational decision. He leaves Antony, once Antony's defeat is sure, and almost immediately has to recognise the emotional error of the choice. He dies, symbolically, of a broken heart. In his fate, we see the nature of the judgements made in the play. Rational decisions disintegrate under emotional pressure; passionate decisions expose the character to destruction by less passionate men.

The relative validity of all human judgements is also closely related to the structure of the play, in which the movement of the action is explicable, to some extent, by Shakespeare's desire to show different judgements of the same event succeeding each other. For instance, what do we feel about Antony's decision to return to Cleopatra such a short time after marrying Octavia? In Act II, Scene iii, the Soothsayer does provide what we might call a psychological reason for leaving Rome. He tells Antony that Caesar's fortunes 'rise higher' and advises:

> Therefore, O Antony, stay not by his side:
> Thy demon, that thy spirit which keeps thee, is
> Noble, courageous, high, unmatchable,
> Where Caesar's is not. But near him, thy angel
> Becomes afeard; as being o'erpower'd, therefore
> Make space enough between you. (II, iii, 17–22)

An objective reason is here given for Antony's departure, but, moments later, Antony formulates his own motives in a quite different way:

> . . . though I make this marriage for my peace,
> I' the east my pleasure lies. (II, iii, 38–9)

Here we feel his personal, sensual concerns asserting themselves. We cannot judge whether Antony's return to Egypt is a recognition of his limitations, or an indulgence of his passions. Nor, really, does he know. Judgements of different kinds succeed each other in time and space. Shakespeare uses the dialectical movement of his play between Rome and Egypt to emphasise the relative quality of the judgements, as well as to create a sense of totality.

While considering these changes in place, it is worth remembering that Shakespeare had in front of him (in North's Plutarch) an historically accurate plan for shifting his characters about the Empire. As usual, though, he foreshortens, omits, compresses and expands historical detail to create the dramatic tensions he wants. All the same, we see another aspect of the ambivalent nature of the play if we remember that it has affinities with the histories as well as with the tragedies. This comes to us mainly in the vision of historical process that the play presents, in the idea of 'fortune' or destiny. Fortune, in *Antony and Cleopatra* is seen, not as a settled, purposive development, but as a fluctuating,

B

ebb-and-flow movement, destructive as well as advantageous. A man's fortune, or success in life, is his reward for taking a fortunate decision and catching the correct movement of this force, which is in the play consistently likened to the tide. Failure to catch or hold the tidal movement leaves a man at the mercy of the return of the tide, and open to the consequent 'rotting' or 'melting', both pervasive images of disintegration. It is this force of Fortune that, more than anything else in the play, is the 'secret cause' of the tragic process, and its fluctuations have their counterparts in the structure and the imagery of the play.

Yet it is important to notice that this Fortune is not conceived of at all as an other-worldly force. It is essentially a force of this terrestrial world, and neither in action nor in imagery is it given any supernatural extension. *Antony and Cleopatra* differs from the other tragedies in its unremitting insistence upon the heroes' fates being decided in the human world, and on the complex quality of life here on earth. It neither suggests nor denies the possibility of an order of the universe existing before and after the tragic events. Rather, Shakespeare concentrates upon creating his human world out of two irreconcilable human forces —Roman duty and Egyptian love—and upon the tragic hero's attempts to reconcile these. Antony is in conflict, not with an order which transcends him morally or spiritually, but with the changing complexities of human existence. His death is not a vindication of an order he has violated, as is Macbeth's; nor is it a vindication of himself for having accepted and executed a commandment emanating from that order, as is Hamlet's. Both his struggle and his death are all-too-human, and open to more ironic interpretation than are the actions of any other Shakespearean tragic hero. None of his actions is tragically authentic; even his death is a bungled affair. Nothing he *does* makes him a tragic figure. Yet, he is undeniably of tragic stature. His power to transcend, in human quality, the forces ranged against him, while they defeat him in fact, lies in his speeches. The poetry given to Antony and to Cleopatra plays a decisive part in our final feeling of the tragedy of the play, and is in its highly-wrought rhetorical quality a distinctive attribute of the play.

First, it is interesting to note that a good deal of the action lies in the poetry. By this I mean that many of the significant choices, conflicts, qualities of the drama are enacted by the poetry alone. We do not see Cleopatra on Cydnus—the scene is described by Enobarbus. Octavius describes several scenes taking place in Egypt; Antony and Cleopatra describe scenes that do, or could, take place in Rome. The entire sequence of battle scenes are described at the time by observers, and by the participants only after the battle is over.

Secondly, as we have seen, the poetry serves to ennoble the protagonists, advancing a movement of feeling contrary to the movement of the action, by which they are defeated and degraded and die. Here, Shakespeare uses his rhetoric to the full; each failure or ignoble action by Antony is balanced with a speech of such poetic quality as to re-engage our sympathy with him at once. Even Cleopatra, as the play goes on, develops this capacity to enlarge her actions by her words, and her final speeches on Antony in Act V, Scene ii, are the climax of this movement in the play. We understand her to be exaggerating, we know that this Antony is only her dream; and if we did not, Dolabella's 'Gentle madam, no' reminds us. Yet the power of the speech is such as to elevate Cleopatra as she speaks it, and give Antony, retrospectively, a glory and a symbolic status to which we would not have given belief at the time. The persuasive moulding power that the poetry exercises over us is a further distinctive quality of this tragedy.

I think, finally, that we may go further and perceive a relation between theme and form that is unique and satisfying in the highest degree. The story of Antony and Cleopatra, as Shakespeare handles it, has as its theme the conflict of the fact with the imagination. Against the nature of their world and their responsibilities *as they are*, the tragic figures can erect, not other worlds and other responsibilities, but only an imaginative perception of a world and a quality of love *that might be*. They assert the truth and vitality of their feelings against the facts of their situations. That, at its broadest, is the theme of the play. The form of the play is an increasing tension between the weight and direction of the action, and the force and contrary direction of the poetry. The action tends to degradation and destruction, the poetry to celebrating the transcendent truth and vitality of the emotions of the protagonists. Thus, returning to Act V, Scene ii, it is to be expected that at the most tragic moment of the action (Antony dead, herself a captive awaiting death or humiliation), Cleopatra should be given the power to force us to reassess our judgements of herself and of Antony. As I will try to show in the following chapters, it is out of such unresolved tensions, ambivalences and perpetual adjustments that the play is created.

2. The Structure of the Play

(i) Events in time and space

What happens in a play comes to pass in a sequence of events arranged one after another in time. Our primary interest in the structure of a play lies in this arrangement of the events in time, because, initially, it is impossible for the audience to respond to any other sequence. In this light, the main narrative line of *Antony and Cleopatra* is quite clear. As a sequence of events in time, it depicts the declining fortunes and subsequent deaths of the tragic figures. The sense of a doomed love is created early in the play, and despite intermittent stands against fate, the end is always felt to be inevitable. Antony may go back to Rome and patch up a peace with Octavius, he may even win one battle; but in our imaginations the plot is dominated by the secret forces of life that have placed Antony and Caesar on opposite, destructive sides. None of the characters can transcend these forces, and, as several critics have observed, 'the play's action progresses steadily towards death'.[1] Yet within this main movement, another pattern is soon felt. This is a pattern of swift alternating movements between Rome and Egypt, with sporadic sorties to other parts of the Empire, as in Act III, Scene i, which editors set on 'a plain in Syria'. The changes in place are associated in the verbal texture of the play with the images of the vacillating tide.

In the play's structure, then, we are made aware of a conflict between an inevitable progress to one point in time (the deaths of the tragic figures) and vacillating progresses between different points in space (the geographical centres of the conflicting attitudes to life). It is a fluid but highly effective structure, and the effectiveness lies in the fluidity of the elements. By ignoring all theories of dramatic construction, and creating a form that embodies the theme of the work, Shakespeare is able to express unobtrusively his central perception: that the final point in time is the result of the swiftly alternating movement between different points in space. The key to understanding the complex unity of the play is once again to grasp a paradoxical idea—that dramatic coherence and solidity can co-exist with the depiction of fluidity and vacillation. It is again one

[1] S. S. Smith, 'This Great Solemnity: the presentation of death in *Antony and Cleopatra*', *English Studies*, April 1964, pp. 163–76

of its really fruitful tensions that we should feel that the play has sim-
ultaneously a unified structure and diverse, conflicting elements within
that structure.

The main tragic movement is also a progressive revelation and
development of character and theme. Each successive act increases our
understanding of the main characters, and does so while they themselves
are changing and developing. They become increasingly conscious of
their doomed position, and this increased consciousness, leading to
agonised assessments of cause and motive, is another means by which we
know more about them. Successive events and crises cause them to
display their inner qualities by their actions, and in this way also our
knowledge of character is controlled by the sequence of events. But if
the play contains a progressive revelation of character and theme, it also
shows the characters involved in a destructive vacillation between in-
compatible alternative choices. Shakespeare emphasises this aspect by
gradually decreasing the intervals between the Roman and Egyptian
scenes, making, as it were, the tragic pendulum swing faster as the end
approaches. At the beginning of the play, the scenes in both Egypt and
Rome are sustained over considerable stage time. As the play progresses,
we switch increasingly quickly from one side to the other, until, in the
battle scenes in Acts III and IV, we are moving every ten or twelve
lines. Such short scenes are appropriate, of course, to the feeling of
confusion and chaos on the battlefield, but they also contribute to
our sense of rapidly approaching destruction. This swift movement is
finally steadied by the long Scene xiv of Act IV. The vacillation is now
ended by the defeat of Antony, who has tried to contain these warring
opposites within his 'visible shape'. The quiet stillness of this scene (and
of Scene xv) is particularly striking after the swift changes from scene
to scene, and the violent action within each scene. Obviously, it is a
stillness suggesting defeat and impending death. The action ceases to
move in space because the tragic heroes—Antony wounded, Cleopatra
locked in her monument—can no longer do so. Yet it is also the stillness
of achieved purpose. Antony *does* finally find a stability within his
shifting personality, if only by the act of death. Extended into the
structure of the play, this paradox accounts for our sense that the lack of
movement from Act IV, Scene xiv, to the end of the play is the stillness
both of defeat and of victory. Finally, the two movements are integrated.
The sequence of events in time reaches its stasis in these scenes, as does
the sequence of events in space.

This aspect of the play is generally recognised today. Our sense that a dramatist is bound by set rules of organisation is mercifully weak, and we are often more satisfied with a unique structure, related to the themes, than with any adherence to external rules. We thus accept quite easily the imaginative demands made on the audience by a play which moves swiftly from place to place, and we understand how well-adapted such a play is to the Elizabethan theatre, where a word, a gesture, a banner or a procession establishes the locality of the scene.

(ii) Control of the audience

There is, however, another aspect of structure which has not been so fully investigated in relation to *Antony and Cleopatra*. This is the way in which the dramatist controls his sequence of events in order to control his audience's responses. In this view, the structure is seen as a carefully contrived way of making the audience feel what they should feel when they should feel it. If we look closely at the structure of *Antony and Cleopatra*, we see this process of control and development of emotional response dictating the placing and intensity of each scene, again with the aim of causing us to experience the fullness of the dramatic situation.

Antony and Cleopatra differs from its source material, and from the other treatments of the story likely to be known to Shakespeare, in ways which clearly show Shakespeare's purposes. The most important of these is the sympathetic treatment given Cleopatra, from which arises the sense, unique to Shakespeare's play, that the 'love' is a genuine alternative to the 'duty'. But the kinds of emphases he makes to create this effect show clearly that Shakespeare starts with the assumption that his audience is more sympathetic to the Roman values, and likely to have a morally disapproving attitude to Cleopatra. Large portions of the play are devoted to re-forming these responses. Considerable attention is given early in the play to diminishing the value of Roman attitudes, while the final acts of the play obviously elevate Cleopatra's value.

The tragic effect Shakespeare achieves also depends upon these responses, since it is through them that he creates the sense that the alternatives facing the tragic hero are of nearly equal strength. This is essential to the tragic effect of the play. If either the Roman or the Egyptian life were obviously preferable, the struggle, and thus the tragic tension, would be lost. To achieve his tragic effect the dramatist has then to re-organise the responses of his audience. How does Shakespeare set about this task?

First, he presents Rome as less than she historically is. We hear virtually nothing of the traditional and valuable Roman attitudes. Political stability, loyalty, courage, patriotism, military resourcefulness are barely mentioned. Instead, Shakespeare begins his process of reduction by emphasising the human coldness and political duplicity of Octavius Caesar, and then extends these characteristics through the whole Empire. Pompey and Ventidius both show awareness of the need for deceit and duplicity, and even Antony—in his Roman dealings—is not above concealing his feelings and motives. Finally, the Roman people—who do not actually appear in the play—are consistently referred to as shifting, vacillating and untrustworthy.

Shakespeare's Octavius Caesar is not at all true to what we know of history's (or even Plutarch's) Octavius. Shakespeare emphasises his qualities of self-interest, remorseless ambition for himself and his Empire, and total unconcern for individuals who stand in the way of his aims. In the course of the play he is responsible for the death of Lepidus, and for the humiliation of his sister and the destruction of her integrity. The callous way in which he disposes of Lepidus is emphasised by the words in which the act is reported by Eros to the audience:

> Caesar, having made use of him in the wars 'gainst Pompey, presently denied him rivality, would not let him partake in the glory of the action, and not resting here, accuses him of letters he had formerly wrote to Pompey; upon his own appeal, seizes him; so the poor third is up, till death enlarge his confine. (III, v, 6–12)

The effect of this perversion of justice is intensified by the hard and cynical tone Eros adopts towards it. Political assassination of this kind, and the cruel opportunism associated with it, lies at the heart of Roman order and power. Antony himself is involved in such processes, as Eros' next comment makes clear:

> He's walking in the garden—thus, and spurns
> The rush that lies before him; cries, 'Fool Lepidus!'
> And threats the throat of that his officer
> That murder'd Pompey. (III, v, 16–19)

The most we can say for Antony here is that he appears to feel remorse, while Caesar's response to Lepidus' fate is quite cold:

> . . . Lepidus was grown too cruel,
> That he his high authority abus'd,
> And did deserve his change: . . . (III, vi, 32–4)

Conversely, before we feel too much sympathy for Pompey, let us remember his own highly equivocal response to Menas's suggestion that he perpetrate a major political assassination himself, by putting his barge to sea and murdering his guests:

> Ah, this thou shouldst have done,
> And not have spoke on't. In me 'tis villainy,
> In thee, 't had been good service . . .
>
> . . . Repent that e'er thy tongue
> Hath so betray'd thine act. Being done unknown,
> I should have found it afterwards well done,
> But must condemn it now . . . (II, vii, 73-9)

In short, Pompey wishes that the murders had been committed. He would be happy to seize the benefits, while avoiding the responsibility. We obviously cannot feel total sympathy for him when he, in turn, becomes a victim of these same attitudes. In fact, both scenes of apparent reconciliation between the warring Roman parties (Act II, Scenes vi and vii) are used by Shakespeare almost entirely to diminish the Romans in our eyes. The negotiations provide only the most transparent cover for the mutual distrust, and the banquet in Scene vii is drab, degrading and joyless. The reason for the inclusion of these scenes can only be to show the flaws beneath the imperial grandeur of Rome. Much the same comment applies to Act III, Scene i. In it, we see Ventidius for the only time in the play. He is brought in solely to make this damaging comment on the military structure of the Empire:

> Who does i' the wars more than his captain can,
> Becomes his captain's captain: and ambition,
> The soldier's virtue, rather makes choice of loss,
> Than gain which darkens him.
> I could do more to do Antonius good,
> But 'twould offend him. And in his offence
> Should my performance perish. (III, i, 21-7)

This perception, rendered flatly and cynically, is obviously realistic, and Ventidius rightly regards this state of affairs as in the nature of his world. Despite one or two references to personal courage and unselfish concern with others (notably in Caesar's speech about Antony in Act I, Scene iv, lines 55-71), the Roman leaders are presented as cold, calculating, unscrupulous and murderous in their pursuit of power. The vaunted stability of the Empire rests upon shifting internal conflicts and intrigues, and here once again the play comes back to that typical sense of an inner fluidity and vacillation contrasting with an external appearance of stability.

We feel this strongly also in the way in which the Roman people are presented. That they are vacillating, untrustworthy, even disloyal, is the only fact Antony and Caesar agree on in the whole play. Antony's hostility to them is personal though understandable:

> . . . Our slippery people,
> Whose love is never link'd to the deserver
> Till his deserts are past, . . . (I, ii, 183–5)

But when Caesar very explicitly corroborates Antony's judgement, we feel disposed to accept it as accurate:

> . . . This common body,
> Like to a vagabond flag upon the stream,
> Goes to, and back, lackeying the varying tide,
> To rot itself with motion. (I, iv, 44–7)

The Roman people are fit to be governed only by the Roman leaders. The unscrupulous lead the untrustworthy. Shakespeare's careful concentration upon this aspect of Roman life, his careful dissection of the Pompey plot, his careful inclusion of Lepidus' death, all serve to create in the audience a deep distrust in the moral value of the Roman Empire. What follows is a willingness to see Egypt more favourably than the Romans ever can. By the beginning of Act III, the assumptions on which we are to judge Rome in this play have been established.

(iii) *Egyptian responses*

The second means Shakespeare uses to re-organise our conventional responses to his story is to make more favourable our judgements of Cleopatra. Once again, the order of scenes and the relation between them makes immediate sense if this aim is kept in mind. Shakespeare first allows the Roman view of her to establish itself in the play. Philo's opening speech, with its 'gypsy' and 'strumpet' judgements, is not immediately contradicted. Indeed, the dominant impression we have of Cleopatra in the first scene is of a coquettish and shallow temptress. Even her subsequent appearances in Act I do not substantially deepen this judgement, though there are some isolated moments of poetic seriousness ('Eternity was in our lips and eyes . . .' and '. . . my oblivion is a very Antony') that hint at depths in her emotion. Working against this deepening is Act I, Scene ii, which economically establishes the gay

laxity in speech and behaviour that is typical of her court, and emphasises
the way in which she herself consciously practises her wiles:

> . . . If you find him sad,
> Say I am dancing; if in mirth, report
> That I am sudden sick . . . (I, iii, 3–5)

It is impossible to be sure of a coherent response to her at this stage, and
any clear demonstration that she transcends the unsympathetic judgement
of the Roman soldiers must wait until Enobarbus' speeches in Act
II, Scene ii. These are the first reliable guides we have on how to judge
her, and contain most of the elements out of which we fashion an attitude
to her during the first four acts. Her combination of royal stateliness
with intense sexuality, languidness with vitality, spontaneity with
deep planning, are magnificently evoked in Enobarbus' speeches. We
give added belief to them as they are spoken by a man not elsewhere very
favourable to Cleopatra.

By the beginning of Act III, we know how to approach Cleopatra,
though not how finally to judge her. Her position in the structure of
Acts II, III and IV is best analysed along the lines of her variousness, her
changeableness. A brief summary of what she does will substantiate this.
In Act II, Scene v, she degrades herself by attacking the messenger bringing news of Antony's marriage, only to recall him in Act III, Scene iii,
and question him seriously and politely. By Act III, Scene vii, she is
reconciled to Antony and insisting upon her right and capacity to play a
part in the war. Her immediate influence is to get Antony to fight by
sea, and, having done so, she betrays him by fleeing from the battle and
drawing him after her. Confronted with Antony's rage, she first argues
back in defence of her action:

> . . . I little thought
> You would have follow'd . . . (III, xi, 55–6)

and then simply, and successfully, begs 'Pardon, pardon'. Once again,
the scene shows her variability. Shakespeare's intention obviously is to
make us feel our inability to reduce her to a single judgement. The same
is true of her subsequent appearances in Acts III and IV. The moral
ambiguity of her reception of Thidias (III, xiii) is quite strong enough to
make us feel that Antony has grounds for suspicion at least. But she
follows it with her strongest and most moving speech of emotional
loyalty (III, xiii, 158–67), with which both Antony and we are 'satisfied'.
In her next sustained scene (IV, iv), we see her buckling on Antony's

armour, and urging him forward into battle, and later, greeting his victorious return in fine poetry:

> Lord of lords,
> O infinite virtue, com'st thou smiling from
> The world's great snare uncaught? (IV, viii, 16–18)

In the next day's battle, however, her fleet finally betrays Antony in the most humiliating way by actually joining Caesar's forces, and Cleopatra is set back in our estimation to the 'triple-turn'd whore' that Antony here names her. Terrified of his rage, she retires to her monument, from which she will send the false news of her death, and so precipitate the tragedy.

Through all this central portion of the play, then, the scenes are so arranged in relation to each other as to deny us a coherent judgement of Cleopatra. She justifies, in some of her actions, the worst judgements the Romans can bring against her. In other actions, and above all in the poetry she speaks, she transcends these judgements, giving evidence of a depth of attachment and a capacity for loyalty which simply cannot be logically reconciled with what she does. Just because of the inevitable ambivalence in our judgements, we already begin to feel hints of her stature, and of the way Shakespeare will raise her above the conventional moral judgements we may initially have made. However, the last four scenes of the play finally put her beyond the judgements of any of the characters, and show us that she can be contained only by the dramatist's imagination—and ours, to the extent that we can follow Shakespeare. In Act V, the qualities of stability, loyalty and courage which we felt existed only in her words, finally issue in action. Not in an unambiguous action, it is true. The careful consideration of painless ways to die, the confusion about the immediate motives for her death, the ambiguous imagery surrounding her death by the bite of the asp—these all complicate our response, make it difficult for us to see her suicide as the tragic assertion of a final choice. Yet, the tragic feeling of the Act is undeniable. Cleopatra finally discovers the power to endure and the power to apprehend her position. Ultimately, she *is* destroyed: but

> as the shadows gather round her, she stands up the more resolutely, she sees the human situation with clearer eyes.[2]

The structural significance of these final scenes is thus again closely related to the tragic effect required by Shakespeare. The disappearance of

[2] Clifford Leech, *Shakespeare's Tragedies*, London, 1950

Antony in Act IV, and Cleopatra's dominance of Act V, is not a case of the dramatist's obsession with a character of his own creation. Rather, along with the careful reduction of Roman values in Acts I and II, it is the structural means by which he causes his audience once again to re-think a complex value situation; to feel their way through it once again. Starting with a realistic appraisal of the assumptions of his audience, Shakespeare uses them by altering and deepening them, and the structure of the play is evidence of this. What Lionel Trilling says of drama in general is true of *Antony and Cleopatra* as well:

> Drama . . . is an arrangement of moral and emotional elements in such a way as to conduct the mind to a certain affective condition . . . The form of the drama is its idea, and its idea is its form.[3]

[3] 'The Meaning of a Literary Idea', *The Liberal Imagination*, London, 1955

3. Central Themes and Images

(i) Theme and imagery in action

Act I, Scene i, is in structure and imagery a microcosm of the play. Contained within the sixty-two lines are the central themes of the play (in their full ambiguity), the most important emotional rhythms of the work, and some of the central imagery. In its structure, the scene presents us with the love of Antony and Cleopatra firmly placed between two judgements of that love. In lines 1–14, Philo gives us a preliminary evaluative description of the relationship; in lines 15–55 we see it for ourselves; and in lines 56–62 Philo and Demetrius reiterate the Roman judgement. The technique is that of the whole play—to confront judgements of reality with the reality itself, and in this way to show what portions of the reality support the judgement, and how much less the judgement is than the reality.

Basically, Philo's speech presents us with a before-and-after picture of his general. Before meeting Cleopatra, Antony embodied all Roman virtues. His captain's heart could scarcely be contained within his armour, his 'goodly' eyes 'glow'd' in his concern with the military front, and unconcern with women's foreheads. Most of the words suggest order, straight lines: 'files', 'musters', 'pillar' and, above all, 'measure'. One of the three rulers of the world, Antony is likened, in his vigour and uprightness, to the god of war, Mars himself. The process of mythologising the tragic hero has begun.

Yet, Philo's speech is equally evocative of the weaknesses within the god-like figure. If he was once upright, his look and posture are now described by the verbs 'bend' and 'turn', and the nouns 'office' (or service) and 'devotion'. The soldier-statesman has become the 'strumpet's fool'. Philo identifies two causes of this change. First, Antony's 'dotage'—a word which combines implications of old age and obsessional passion. Secondly, his incapacity to practise self-restraint, suggested in 'o'erflows the measure' and 'reneges all temper'. In the way Philo puts his criticisms, the Roman values appear clearly. Military prowess, stern leadership, stability of purpose, self-restraint; by these standards Antony is degrading himself, and Cleopatra is a 'gypsy' and a 'strumpet'. In Philo's speech we have the first of which L. C. Knights calls 'different and apparently irreconcilable evaluations of the central experience'.

Then we see the 'central experience' for ourselves. In forty lines, Shakespeare evokes most of the strengths and weaknesses of their love, showing what there is in it that gives force to Philo's criticisms, and what there is that he cannot see. The first four lines the lovers speak are almost an antiphonal chant, and evoke a sense of total immersion in each other. Neither notices nor greets any other character, and the messenger has to intrude his presence on them. In the exchange, Cleopatra is conquettishly contradictory, demanding an assertion of how much Antony loves her, and then denying that he has the right to love her that much. Antony is romantically serious, especially in his second line where he asserts, in an almost dogged tone, the transcendental quality of their love. How tragically true it is that the world cannot contain the lovers, he cannot yet know.

Into this inner world, Roman duty intrudes, and Cleopatra takes the opportunity of taunting Antony with subservience to the 'scarce-bearded Caesar' and 'shrill-tongued Fulvia'. Antony responds again at a much deeper level, and his speech rejecting his Roman life and position focuses the central comparisons of the play. The solidity, size and scope of the Empire are evoked—especially in 'wide arch' and 'rang'd'—and, as he embraces her, the Roman concerns are contrasted with his love. The material Roman world is, at this moment, almost bestial ('dungy', 'beast') compared to the emotional quality of his love. The speech generates great sympathy for Antony, which he almost immediately dissipates by swinging from this depth of feeling to the purely sensual tone of:

> There's not a minute of our lives should stretch
> without some pleasure now. What sport tonight?

He exits with a discourteous refusal to speak to the messenger.

We can see that there is enough in his conduct to appal the Romans. And Shakespeare, giving his scene a fine circularity, allows them to express their horror. Yet, how much more there is—in Antony at least—than they can see. The conviction and beauty of his responses elude their judgements. A double ambivalence is immediately created —first, between our judgement and Philo's, and then within the reality we are judging. The scene also presents the conflict of personal satisfactions and impersonal duty that is within Antony himself, and does so in two sets of images characteristic of the play. The Roman life is associated with images of straightness and stability, the Egyptian with images of fluidity ('o'erflows'), mingling ('stirr'd') and relaxation ('soft hours'). These patterns are projected through the play. The integration of theme and image in the actual dramatic movement of the scene provides an example of how this works over the whole play.

(ii) Themes

Accepting the idea that the meaning of a drama lies in our experience of the whole play in enactment, we will find only a limited utility in defining the themes of a play. The action, the relations between the characters, and the poetry will extend and deepen, at all points in the play, any formulation of theme-in-the-abstract that we may produce. On the other hand, in analysing a play it often proves useful to be able to say to oneself 'Eventually what the play is about is: . . .', and then have a workably small group of ideas on which to focus.

The central theme of *Antony and Cleopatra* is the conflict between a flawed love and an all-consuming duty. The terms in which this is put might be altered or refined. One might say something more vague like 'personal satisfaction' for love, and 'commitment to the state' for duty, but the essential point of a conflict between the private and public spheres of life remains. Yet, obviously this is not a conflict between any love and any duty at any time. In Antony's fate is involved a unique combination of factors. His love for Cleopatra would not seem such a gross neglect of duty if he were not one of the triumvirate, or if the triumvirate were not the rulers of the Roman Empire. Nor would it be so dangerous if Octavius Caesar were not his political rival. Similarly, the love for Cleopatra is also unique. In the first instance, Shakespeare's interest in the story is because of its unique qualities, and it is these that we experience first. The imaginative extensions by which we come to regard it as a typical human experience follow later.

Secondly, it is not the two alternatives, nor either one of them, that is the theme, but rather the conflict between them. Antony is torn between the alternative ways of life, and the drama centres upon his awareness of the values (and failings) of each. From this, it must also centre on his desire to unite the qualities of each within his life and personality. The play makes us feel how it is inevitable that he should attempt this grand gesture, and inevitable that he should fail.

From this it will follow that ambivalence is not the theme of the play, but rather the medium in which the play moves. Here again further distinctions are helpful. Ambivalence is the most important quality of the

world which is created in the drama. We do not rightly know what are
the dominant aspects of that world. In this case, the ambivalence is a
destructive quality, because it makes it impossible for the characters to
identify anything solid upon which they can build their lives.

Ambivalence is also the dominant mode of perception in the play.
Shakespeare deliberately refuses us a single, unified viewpoint on an
already ambivalent reality. In this case, the ambivalence is creative, since
it forces us to expand, modify and even suspend some of our conventional moral and emotional attitudes as we respond to a vision of life
that is far greater than our own.

From these ideas it follows again that a subsidiary theme in the play
concerns judgement. To state it simply, the play demonstrates the
relative quality of all human judgements. The reality that is to be judged
shifts too quickly and too often for judgements of it to be anything but
partial and temporary. The 'inner reality' of the play—that which is
experienced as reality by the characters—displays shifting ambivalent
qualities. So does the 'outer reality'—that which is experienced as
reality by the audience watching the play. Consequently, we observe
enacted before us a story in which the characters betray themselves by
making partial judgements; but we are also aware that our own judgements on the action are partial and imperfect.

The case of Octavia illustrates clearly these shifting judgements.
Her part in the story is to attempt to unite Caesar and Antony, at the
time when their basic division is entirely clear. Her role begins as that of
a Roman matron participating in a normal political marriage. At least,
Agrippa presents it in this way:

> To hold you in perpetual amity,
> To make you brothers, and to knit your hearts
> With an unslipping knot, take Antony
> Octavia to his wife; . . . (II, ii, 125–8)

On these terms, both men grasp it—indeed, the tone suggests that they
grasp at it. Antony proclaims:

> May I never
> To this good purpose, that so fairly shows,
> Dream of impediment . . . (II, ii, 144–6)

Caesar is even more lofty in his sentiments:

> Let her live
> To join our kingdoms, and our hearts, and never
> Fly off our loves again . . . (II, ii, 151–3)

Antony actually makes an attempt to give some emotional depth to the political reality:

> My Octavia,
> Read not my blemishes in the world's report:
> I have not kept my square, but that to come
> Shall all be done by the rule. Good night, dear lady. (II, iii, 4–7)

However, Enobarbus soon sees another reality—that Octavia will intensify rather than remove conflict, and will herself become the cause of further conflict:

> But you shall find the band that
> seems to tie their friendship together will be the
> very strangler of their amity . . . (II, vi, 117–19)

Antony gives a further hint of enmity within friendship in bidding farewell to Caesar:

> I'll wrestle with you in my strength of love: (III, ii, 63)

But it is an image that he uses slightly earlier that shows us that the reality of Octavia's position is not what we first took it to be:

> Her tongue will not obey her heart, nor can
> Her heart inform her tongue—the swan's down feather,
> That stands upon the swell at the full of tide,
> And neither way inclines. (III, ii, 47–50)

Octavia's soft, defenceless quality and inevitable destruction are suggested by the image of the feather, and her uselessness as a force to bind the ever-moving tide is clear. The image of the tide catches up both the way in which previous judgements will be proved wrong (she will not bind them together), and the idea that the reality they purported to judge defies them by its fluidity. We come back again to the vacillation and perpetual change which characterises the play.

(iii) *Patterns of images*

We saw in analysing structure that a dialectic of action was an important aspect of the play. A second structure giving coherence to the play is the dialectic of imagery, which also centres around Rome and Egypt.

Egypt—and Cleopatra—are constantly associated with images of the moon and water. The water images arise naturally from Egypt's dependence upon the Nile (and especially upon its annual and uncontrollable flooding), for fertile soil, crops and thus life itself. The moon images arise from Cleopatra's mythical association with Isis who, as a contemporary writer tells us, 'is nothing else but the moon'.[1] From these sources, first Plutarch, and then Shakespeare, creates a configuration of images that suggests her contradictory qualities. The Nile's flooding contains potential destruction as well as fertility, and the moon (in its never-changing course and ever-changing shape) combines ideas of permanence and variability. In the images of mud and slime, a quality of degradation is associated with Egypt, but this is offset again by suggestions that life itself originates in that mud. The asp, a snake living in the riverside slime, becomes yet another variable image, containing suggestions of sexual potency as well as death, and even, in Act V, Scene ii, linking itself to ideas of maternity already associated with Cleopatra. It is obviously fitting that the military activities of the Egyptians should be by sea.

The second basic pattern of images associates Rome with the earth or land. Again, this pattern has a factual, even historical, basis. Rome's military genius was essentially expressed in the foot-soldier. This pattern begins as early as Antony's first speech, in which Roman 'earth' and 'clay' are opposed to the emotional quality of his Egyptian love. Through this association we feel the stability and solidity of the Roman world. The clearest expression of this combination is given in a speech by an unnamed soldier:

> O noble Emperor, do not fight by sea,
> Trust not to rotten planks . . .
> . . . Let the Egyptians
> And the Phoenicians go a-ducking; we
> Have us'd to conquer standing on the earth,
> And fighting foot to foot. (III, vii, 61-6)

As the tone of this passage suggests, Roman moral attitudes are basically stoical—they endure rather than suffer. When Antony wishes to find an image of moral perception, he turns naturally to the earth:

> O then we bring forth weeds,
> When our quick minds lie still, and our ills told us
> Is as our earing . . . (I, ii, 106-8)

Later in the drama, he chooses the same terms to express his loss of leadership:

[1] Michael Lloyd, 'Cleopatra as Isis', *Shakespeare Survey*, Vol. XII, 1959

> Hark, the land bids me tread no more upon 't,
> It is asham'd to bear me. Friends, come hither:
> I am so lated in the world that I
> Have lost my way for ever. I have a ship,
> Laden with gold, take that, divide it; fly, . . . (III, xi. 1–5)

Between these opposing images of water and earth, Shakespeare creates a series of images of the processes of change. The most important of these are images of earth melting into water, and finally water mingling with water. Antony first suggests this pattern in his 'Let Rome in Tiber melt . . .', giving us an image of the dissolution of part of his life. Cleopatra echoes this as, with the news of his marriage to Octavia, she despairs of their love:

> Melt Egypt into Nile! and kindly creatures
> Turn all to serpents! . . . (II, v, 78–9)

These, and other images of dissolution, are closely associated with the images of the vacillating tide discussed in Chapter 1, and with the images of rotting and disintegrating that Caesar has used about the Roman people. This pattern of images reinforces the sense of dissolution by perpetual movement between conflicting opposites that is so important a part of the structure.

When these ideas are translated into Antony's internal struggle, they are expressed more often in images of melting. As early as the Thidias scene in Act III, Scene xii, Antony proclaims:

> Authority melts from me . . . (line 90),

and in Act IV, Scene xii, after the final defeat, he is given a speech of great imagistic complexity built around the idea of melting:

> Fortune and Antony part here, even here
> Do we shake hands. All come to this? The hearts
> That spaniel'd me at heels, to whom I gave
> Their wishes, do discandy, melt their sweets
> On blossoming Caesar: and this pine is bark'd,
> That overtopp'd them all. . . . (IV, xii, 19–24)

The images of this speech are characteristically paradoxical. The 'spaniel'd' links with 'bark'd', in the sense that the fawning dogs have now turned hostile; while 'bark'd' (in its other sense of 'to strip') links obviously with the image of growth in 'blossoming Caesar'. The 'triple pillar of the world' is hinted at in 'this pine', in which there are also several connotations. At the centre of the speech there is again the image of melting, in 'discandy' and 'melt their sweets'. The images suggest that the loyalty of Antony's followers is being turned away from him and towards Caesar; though there is possibly the idea that transferring loyalty in this way destroys the quality of that loyalty ('their sweets melt'), a sentiment obviously appropriate in the case of Enobarbus.

Imagery of melting again dominates Antony's opening speech in Act IV, Scene xiv, where it is used to illustrate what the editor of the Arden edition calls 'man's unstable hold of his very entity'. Antony compares his sense of his own existence—even of his physical existence—to the tenuous stability of clouds drifting into clouds, and finally water mingling with water. He refers to this ever-shifting attempt to define the personality as a 'pageant', suggesting a moving spectacle or show without substantial reality. In the phrase 'the rack dislimns' (Arden editor: 'the drifting clouds efface') similarities of sound suggest that he is undergoing almost a physical disintegration as a result of torture—being torn limb from limb on the rack.

Thus, Antony's tragic end is associated with these images of dissolution and decay because of an inability to hold a steady purpose or a steady view of himself. A further ambivalence occurs when we consider that the images surrounding Cleopatra's death are conversely of steadiness and constancy. In Act V, Scene ii, she returns continuously to this theme. She seeks

> That thing that ends all other deeds,
> Which shackles accidents, and bolts up change (lines 5–6)

She rejects the 'fleeting moon' as her planet, and seeks to be 'Marble-constant'. In the patterns of images it is appropriate that this duality should persist to the end. For Antony, the Roman, death follows upon dissolution. For Cleopatra, the Egyptian, death follows upon the loss of the capacity to change.

4. *The Characters*

(i) *Analysis of characterisation*

Some caution must be used in writing of character as an element of
drama. The critic must beware of abstracting the character from the
texture and movement of the whole play, and considering it as a separate
entity. There is also the lesser danger of regarding the character as we
might a person we know in real life, and applying to it standards of
judgement that are inappropriate to characters in literature. These
unhelpful attitudes are by no means found only in relatively inexperi-
enced students of literature. Critics of stature have sometimes tended to
give this abstracting emphasis to the study of character as well, and to
show frustration if the character does not behave as the critic thinks he
should. Much of the moral disapprobation of Antony originates in this
sort of attitude.

Before looking at the characters of the play, then, it will be useful to
remind ourselves of some guidelines in analysing character. First, we
can agree to concentrate upon the characters-in-conflict, or as they
interact with each other in the drama. With the exception of the
soliloquy, all we know of a character arises from this interaction, and as
there is not a single true soliloquy in *Antony and Cleopatra*, we know
these characters only in conflict.

Secondly, we must bear in mind that the purposes and aims of the
whole work condition and limit the scope of action of the individual
character. These aspects also limit the critic's response, making irrelevant
questions as to what the character might have done if he (or the circumstances) had been different. Rather, we need to concentrate on the
purposes of the dramatist in making the character do what he does, and
not something else. The dramatist chooses events to reveal character,
and choices made by the character always contain potential irony,
since they are by implication choices that exclude some opportunities
even while they grasp others.

Once again, then, the critic must proceed with tact. We should avoid
abstraction when dealing with characters, and yet the abstractions of
'meaning' and 'structure' are always changing and controlling the
creation of individual characters, as well as the audience's response to

them. These necessarily contradictory qualities—the human reality of the character as well as his purpose in an unreal drama—have to be balanced continuously.

(ii) *A Roman thought*

We have already seen that, as a group, the Roman characters are presented as narrow in their desires of life, and unscrupulous in the methods they use to attain even those limited desires. Octavius Caesar epitomises these characteristics, and he is the only one of the four major characters who does not show development or change in the course of the drama. Our first knowledge of him is gained in Act I, Scene iv, and the uncomprehending and censorious attitude to Antony he shows there, persists throughout the play. He appears to soften momentarily in the final scene: but even that grudging acknowledgement of a dimly-discerned quality in Antony that he himself lacks, has been felt in the first scene. Having recounted Antony's exploits in the campaign against Hirtius and Pansa, he concludes:

> . . . and all this—
> It wounds thine honour that I speak it now—
> Was borne so like a soldier, that thy cheek
> So much as lank'd not . . . (I, iv, 68–71)

Caesar is always the politician, able to turn events and personalities to his own advantage—witness how he uses the threat of Pompey to bring Antony back to Rome, and then uses the presence of Antony to subdue Pompey. Naturally, he survives both. He is the master of the time, ignoring Antony's plea that he become

> a child o' the time (II, vii, 98)

or, in other words, immerse himself in the quality of experience at the moment. His refusal to risk spontaneous action, or even statement, is emphasised often in the play. The manœuvring for position on the stage when he and Antony first meet (II, ii, 26–30), is followed by his refusal to commit himself over Agrippa's suggestion until he has heard Antony's response. Then only does he proclaim his delight. On the stage, the careful duplicity would be obvious.

Caesar is obsessed with power and political business. Nowhere is this more clearly seen than in his response to Antony's death. Having spoken slightly more than is required of him (the speech in Act V, Scene i, does contain some emotion behind the formal regret), he is patently glad to be interrupted by a messenger bringing fresh news. When he returns to the subject of Antony's death, his concern is to vindicate his part in the conflict between them. We are not surprised to learn that he has kept detailed records of his correspondence; nor that these letters show *him* to be the wronged party. Even while he is intent on showing that he is not responsible for Antony's death, he is plotting Cleopatra's humiliation—as, indeed, he had previously plotted Antony's murder (III, xii, 20–3).

Some critics see a softening in Caesar at the end,[1] but it seems to me that he shows no more insight into the quality of the lovers at the end than at any other time. His 'recognition' of Cleopatra's 'strong toil of grace' follows immediately upon a factual observation that poison would have caused her to swell, and is uttered in much the same tone. His final speech, especially

> . . . their story is
> No less in pity than his glory which
> Brought them to be lamented . . . (V, ii, 359–61)

is concerned as much with himself as with the lovers, and provides nothing like, say, the spontaneous recognition of a different quality of life that Fortinbras gives to Hamlet.

(iii) *The plain dealer*

In his discussion of types of character in drama, Northrop Frye provides us with a category that includes Enobarbus, at least in some of his aspects:

> . . . a tragic counterpart of the comic refuser of festivity may be discerned in a tragic type of plain dealer who may be simply a faithful friend of the hero, like Horatio in *Hamlet*, but is often an outspoken critic of the tragic action, like Kent in *King Lear* or Enobarbus in *Antony and Cleopatra*. Such a character is in the position of refusing, or at any rate resisting, the tragic movement towards catastrophe.[2]

This is an accurate summary of Enobarbus' position until he leaves Antony. In several early scenes, he has been established as detached from the concerns of the other characters. His tone to Antony is ironic and wittily familiar ('Under a compelling occasion let women die . . .' is a

[1] Richard C. Harrier, 'Cleopatra's End', *Shakespeare Quarterly*, vol. XIII, 1962, pp. 63–5

[2] *Anatomy of Criticism*, p. 218

good example—I, ii, 134–41). Yet he is also given the lyrical evocation of Cleopatra's variousness by which most audiences remember her. As we have seen, he is never taken in by the Octavia machinations, perceiving the fatal flaw in it from the start. He is opposed, rightly, to Cleopatra's participation in the wars (III, vii), and incurs her hostility by saying so openly. In the same scene, he sees the tactical error Antony makes in deciding to fight by sea. Most importantly, he perceives why Antony does this, and the futility of this and Antony's other gesture of challenging Caesar to personal combat:

> . . . that he should dream,
> Knowing all measures, the full Caesar will
> Answer his emptiness; Caesar, thou hast subdued
> His judgement too. (III, xiii, 34–7)

As Enobarbus accurately judges, Caesar lacks altogether the chivalric gesture, and is thus bound to win. But Enobarbus' own tragedy is involved in the same perception. At heart a Roman, he underestimates the power of a gesture to gain a hold over his imagination and thus his loyalty. Like Cleopatra, he feels the quality of Antony only when it is too late. Having taken his rational decision, the Roman basis of which is suggested by the imagery of the 'square', he decides to leave Antony:

> Mine honesty, and I, begin to square.
> The loyalty well held to fools does make
> Our faith mere folly . . . (III, xiii, 41–3)

However, Antony makes his magnanimous response of returning Enobarbus' treasure and sending forgiving messages. The audience actually witnesses this (Act IV, Scene v), and it is then told, in a less moving fashion, to Enobarbus. At that moment, Enobarbus ceases to be the 'plain dealer', and his fate is involved in the tragic movement. He can no longer resist recognising his emotional loyalty to Antony, but the recognition comes when he can no longer give effect to it in action. We might even say that the final movement of the tragedy begins with his death, upon which Shakespeare bestows some care, giving it an almost symbolic significance. Once again, it is part of the ambivalent quality of the play—discoveries by which you might live come at the moment when you have made it impossible to live by them—and serves as a prelude to the main tragic deaths. The images of his final speech (IV, ix, 12–23) echo those of Antony's later. He calls on the moon to witness his plight, and upon the night to 'dispunge' poison on him, in a

way that reminds us of Antony's 'discandy'. Like Cleopatra, he finds that
a power he had considered negligible in his affairs surprises him into
dying. His death, through these similarities, is a prelude to theirs.
Shakespeare gains great pathos by bringing Enobarbus out of the role
of the 'plain dealer' at the end, and I think that we must judge this to be
an advance over the rather lame final couplets given to Kent in *King
Lear*, and even over the way Horatio remains the reporter of events to
the end.

(iv) *A time for words*

The end of Act II provides a pause in the play, enabling us to assess
our responses to the characters of Antony and Cleopatra at this point.
We have seen them together, surrounded by the dubious aura of their
love; and we have seen them separately, acting in distinctively Roman
or Egyptian fashion. More importantly, perhaps, Antony has made his
tragic commitment to the East (II, iii, 37–9), and the process of tragic
decline can begin. This process I will analyse in the next two sections;
here we are concerned with the impression of the two lovers we receive
in the first two acts.

The first response I have already discussed in Chapter 3, showing the
inner and outer reality of the love to be quite different. What Antony
and Cleopatra feel inwardly contrasts with the judgement made by the
Romans on their feelings. The double ambivalence we feel in the first
scene continues through most of the first act. The audience is concerned
at the great difference between the various assessments of the love,
though more favourable to the lovers than the Romans are. At the same
time, Cleopatra's attitudes seem to be less than true love, and we have
seen that Antony does not appear to observe this. We are also concerned
at his ungracious refusal to listen to the messengers. However, in Scene
ii, he changes his mind, summons the messenger back, and then receives
the news of Fulvia's death. His speech after that (I, ii, 119–27) focuses his
mood at this moment.

There are two elements to this speech: the personal and the general.
The shock of Fulvia's death reinforces Antony's need to break out of
Cleopatra's sphere of influence, and take up his responsibilities in the
Roman world. But this is because of the 'ills' hatching there in his
absence, not because of any moral disapproval of Cleopatra. Fulvia's
death also provokes Antony to the kind of general statement that is
typical of the play. He perceives, fleetingly, that we do not value what

we have until we have taken steps to rid ourselves of it. This is a truth both Enobarbus and Cleopatra experience later. Antony does not, characteristically, apply this insight to himself. He reflects on the changing aspirations and circumstances which mock any settled course of action—and then, with Roman briskness, decides upon a settled course of action. Shakespeare causes this display of purposiveness to be further undercut by allowing Antony to endure some fifty lines of Enobarbus' witticisms about Cleopatra before the final orders are issued. Antony shows here the tragic characteristic of perceiving inevitable courses of action, while mentally excepting himself from them. We feel strongly his confusion and concern; the certainty of the first scene ('the nobleness of life/Is to do thus . . .') is entirely dissipated. The audience is once again involved in a re-assessment of the character, and this process is continued in the lively exchange between the two in Scene iii.

Here, both reveal what I might call the 'tactical' and the 'genuine' levels of response. Antony's tactics are to seek for the least troublesome method of telling Cleopatra that he is going to leave her. Cleopatra is intent on preventing him telling her, as well as on postponing his departure. For instance, the brittle tone of Cleopatra's speeches in lines 13–31—in which Antony manages only some twenty words—changes subtly over lines 32–3. The seriousness of her attachment and her heart-sickness at his departure show through the falling cadence of 'when you sued staying'; and the other lines of this speech recall the imagery Antony used earlier to describe their love.

This process is repeated twice more in the scene. Antony, having made one most correct Roman speech (41–56), begins to repeat it, when he is surprised by his feeling into a really convincing oath of loyalty:

> By the fire
> That quickens Nilus' slime, I go from hence
> Thy soldier, servant, making peace or war,
> As thou affects. (68–71)

Cleopatra promptly mocks him. Again, the swift changes of tone cause changes in our assessment of the characters. The same comments might be developed concerning lines 82–101, where Cleopatra's mockery gives way to a genuine feeling. The characters are deliberately employing different levels of response towards each other, and being surprised into still others, not intended. For the audience, it is as if different aspects of each character, and of the situation, are shown in succession, while the pattern of which they are aspects is not yet known to us.

The remaining scenes of Acts I and II present the lovers separately, and further complicate our responses. Cleopatra, especially, acts in ways that largely alienate our sympathies. This is a typical critical response:

> During Antony's absence, Cleopatra's behaviour is self-characterising. She evinces no interest in the business he is engaged in; she is concerned as to what he may be thinking of her, is enveloped in thoughts physical and sensual, and reviews the list of her great lovers . . . She revels in memories of her behaviour to Antony . . .[3]

This summary falls short of the reality of the scenes, because it ignores the poetic quality in what Cleopatra says. Once again, it is this aspect which deepens and gives worth to the actions described, and increases our sympathy with the character. Consider, for instance, Cleopatra's speech in Act I, Scene v, in which she mentions several of the attitudes Mills lists. The wit of the sexual allusions (line 21), the mythic stature she is already beginning to attribute to Antony (23), the half-mocking self-criticism (27–9), and the disarming pleasure in memories (especially the sexual pun on 'die' in line 34): these all give a verbal vitality to her speech that makes its effect on us much more sympathetic than Mills allows.

Surely, the same is true of the exchange with the messenger in Act II, Scene v. The fluctuations of emotion, and the vigour of the responses, offset the tyrannical and unreasonable actions, though they do not cancel them out. We have again to hold both in mind in our response to her. Also Cleopatra is kept before us in a much more flattering way, through Enobarbus's description of her (II, ii, 190–240). Here, the ironic, pragmatic Roman soldier evokes her queenliness and royal dignity, the sense of the completely female world she inhabits, and the lavish show that borders on a repulsive lushness. Taken together with the other speeches I have mentioned, a character of great depth, variety and sympathetic quality is evoked. Yet it remains true that she is capable of unreasonable cruelty, and that much of her activity *is* self-regarding. At this stage, we cannot expect a reconciliation of these opposites.

Much the same might be said of our impressions of Antony. Having sworn love to Cleopatra, and an immediate return, he agrees to marry Octavia and appears to intend never to return. He enters into Roman affairs with spirit and skill. Indeed, as Arnold Stein says in the study quoted previously, at this stage of the play, Antony shows character-

---

[3] L. J. Mills, 'Cleopatra's Tragedy', *Shakespeare Quarterly*, Vol. XI, Spring 1960, pp. 147–62

istics of manliness and self-confidence, the confidence revealing itself
subtly in admissions of error and weakness, as well as in magnanimous
gestures. He shows both these in the exchange with Pompey, when he is
reminded of favours done in the past (II, vi, 46–52). As we will see, much
of Antony's tragic decline is focused for us in his loss of confidence and
decreasing shows of magnanimity—

> that authentic generosity of imagination that shapes with spontaneous
> grace the superior response to ordinary and immediate concerns.[4]

(v) *Greatness going off*

Acts III and IV trace Antony's fall. At the beginning of Act III, he is
apparently at the height of his fortunes, reconciled with Caesar, and once
again playing his part in Roman affairs. In the thirteen scenes of Act III,
he declines from this position to that of a doomed man, with a rapidity
that can only be rendered by the greatest fluidity of staging. Shakespeare
obviously had this swift, destructive sweep in mind, because he left
out much dramatic material from his sources which illuminates Octavia,
but which would have slowed up Antony's tragedy. As it now stands,
we get the sense that no sooner has Octavia left Rome than she is back
again, having been deserted by Antony. Yet, against this movement,
Antony makes the stands, the gestures he judges to be required; and
perhaps the best way to grasp these acts is to concentrate upon these
gestures. Sometimes the gesture increases the speed of his defeat, as in
Act III, Scene vii, where Antony decides to fight by sea at Actium. The
decision is purely a romantic gesture ('For that (Caesar) dares us to 't.'
III, vii, 29); and, as yet, these gestures do not have the authority they
develop later. Indeed, the result here is mainly to emphasise the growing
isolation of Antony from his men. Enobarbus and Canidius argue reason-
ably against the decision. Antony simply rejects their arguments without
reason. He is not even prepared to consider the emotional appeal of the
soldier, which brings into play some of the basic image-patterns of the
work. This speech generates deep resonance through its connection with
the land-sea imagery, and we cannot fail to see the petulance and irre-
sponsibility in Antony's answer. In Scene xi we see the inevitable result:
Antony, having betrayed his own military judgement and his responsibility to his men, is in turn betrayed by Cleopatra. In this scene, too,
we see for the first time that Antony is conscious of a dissolution of his
personality, as the various elements in it begin to fail him. Yet, Cleopatra

[4] Stein, *op. cit.*, p. 590

is still able to lead him through a total revolution of feeling within the
scene, and he ends by scorning the Fortune to which he had felt entirely
subordinate at the beginning. We see this to be a characteristic movement
of feeling at this stage of the play. Antony first takes the blame entirely
upon himself; his first speech contains no statement about Cleopatra's
part in the defeat, though we know that she is almost entirely to blame.
When she finally speaks to him, his response is emotionally complex:

> Egypt, thou knew'st too well,
> My heart was to thy rudder tied by the strings,
> And thou should'st tow me after. O'er my spirit
> Thy full supremacy thou knew'st, and that
> Thy beck might from the bidding of the gods
> Command me. (57–61)

Antony here admits that it was her power over him that caused him to
flee the battle, and that the love is thus a source of weakness. Yet, at the
same time, that the love could bring that about makes it a source of
power as well, again creating a typical ambivalent response. We have a
'brute fact' of weakness overlaid by a 'lyric imagination' of emotional
response working through the rhetoric of the poetry, and the combination almost persuades us that weakness is strength. Antony follows
this gesture with another of forgiveness, and the love has again survived
and even been fortified by failure. Only the call for wine, and the
despairing courage of the final couplet—with the stagey rhetoric of the
poetry—flaw the moment.

Scene xiii, however, focuses our attention on precisely this failing.
Here, in the treatment of Thidias, Antony shows that he can no longer
control his rage and frustration. We understand that the violence of his
commands arises from the suspicion that he does *not* actually command.
In Scene xi, he has stated 'I have lost command' (line 23), and here his
'Authority melts from me', reminds us of this. His final speeches in this
scene reinforce the theme of despair. When he calls upon his 'sad cap-
tains', he shows a knowledge of how things are going, and in one image,
he conveys the inauthentic quality of the gaiety and hope he feels here:

> . . . tonight I'll force
> The wine peep through their scars . . .
> There's sap in it yet. . . . (191–2)

Once again, the rhetorical poetry gives the moment a certain grandeur.
But beneath it, the tragic movement continues, as it does through the
scenes of Act IV.

In the scenes between Antony and Cleopatra in this act, there is a gradual preparation for the mythic status they will finally accord one another. The moments at which they touch upon these aspects are also the moments at which they arrest the tragic decline. Feast succeeds feast in this act, giving a peculiar gaiety to it. Even Caesar is infected and prepared to give the 'waste' of the army to his men (IV, xii, 13–15). Antony is more positive:

> Be bounteous at our meal (IV, ii, 10)

is followed by the drinking of

> carouses to the next day's fate (IV, viii, 34)

This gaiety enters into the lovers' relationship as well. Antony is pleased to allow Cleopatra to dress him in his armour, and gains confidence from this:

> O love,
> That thou could'st see my wars to-day, and knew'st
> The royal occupation, thou should'st see
> A workman in 't. (IV, iv, 15–18)

Cleopatra later responds to this assertion of royal quality with poetry of the same mixture of mythic elaboration and gaiety:

> Lord of lords,
> O infinite virtue, com'st thou smiling from
> The world's great snare uncaught? (IV, viii, 16–18)

Even the loss of Enobarbus embodies, from Antony's side, a gesture of generosity and forgiveness. Act IV combines the inevitable approach of defeat with moments of gaiety and moments of nobility that fill us with the deepest regret at what must be destroyed.

It is not until the final defeat as a result of Cleopatra's treachery, that Antony's sense of his own identity finally collapses. However, the process has been going on throughout the act. Antony has built his identity upon two beliefs about himself—his prowess as a soldier and leader, and his love for Cleopatra. Now, with the loss of his final battle, all that supported him is destroyed. His capacity to define himself by his office, his personal qualities and his relationship with another person has been reduced to nothing. The definite lines of his personality waver, and his sense that

> there is left us
> Ourselves to end ourselves. . . . (IV, xiv, 21–2)

suffuses the scene. Antony's response to the actual news of Cleopatra's
death is one of the most moving speeches in Shakespeare. The long
vowels in

> Unarm, Eros, the long day's task is done (IV, xiv, 35)

stretch the line out into a cry of hopelessness and resignation. The
following images drawn from his now closed life as a soldier extend the
pathos. The sense of loss in 'the torch is out', and aimlessness in 'stray no
further', reach finality of decision in 'seal then, and all is done'.

But the traditional Roman suicide is botched. Antony again comes
close to losing our sympathy by this act, and by stepping outside the
conventions of the tragedy to have, as it were, two death scenes. The
violation of the pattern is only vindicated by what Shakespeare manages
to achieve with the second scene.

(vi) *A Roman by a Roman*

Act IV, Scene xv, contains the parting of the lovers and the death of the
tragic hero. In a manner typical of this drama, the hero does not play
the main part in his own death scene. Subtly, Shakespeare begins the
process of shifting our attention to Cleopatra by giving her a more
important role in this scene. Indeed, most of what Antony himself says
also directs our attention to her, to her royal qualities ('I am dying,
Egypt, dying'), and to his concern with her. Except for his final speech
on fortitude and love, the scene is hers.

Yet, we must not because of this underestimate the visual and emotional effect of Antony's dying. The spectacle of human death always
commands attention on the stage, and our sympathy for Antony
throughout the play has been such that, at his death, the sense of tragic
waste is strong. The qualities of Roman fortitude and stoic endurance
are stressed in the final speech, and yet these qualities are explicitly
related to his love for Cleopatra. The Roman death appears reconciled
with the Egyptian aims of life. But this reconciliation is only apparent.
We understand that Antony has failed to bring together the two worlds
in which he has tried to live. The attempt to span both life-styles has
given Antony his stature, but it is also the cause of his destruction. The
reconciliation of his life as a soldier (expressed here in his honourable
death) with his life as a lover (expressed here in his remaining true to the
death) comes in the moment of dying. As a solution to a certain problem
in life, it is, of course, immediately negated by his death. To grasp this

final paradox is essential to understanding the tragic mood of the play.

Cleopatra's role in this scene again reminds us how open these two characters are to an ironic view. For her whole magnificent verbal celebration founders on two facts—that her lying message is the cause of Antony's death, and that despite all she says, she is too afraid to come down from the Monument. Her first lines evoke a sense of impending universal disaster—but this does not warrant taking the risk of opening the doors of her retreat! These ironies must be borne in mind as we look at what she says.

As Antony dies, Cleopatra's response is expressed in one of the recurrent images of the play:

> The crown o' the earth doth melt . . . (line 63)

She follows this with images of withering, of reduction in value, and of transitoriness (the moon). She ends with a speech that heralds the first appearance of characteristics that will dominate Act V. She begins to show a concern for the feelings of her women, and achieves a vision of herself as

> No more but e'en a woman . . .

thereby linking her fate with that of all women suffering the loss of love. These qualities of concern for others, and a sense of the humanity of her position, do much to sustain her in her final trials. So also do the Roman values she eventually calls upon:

> . . . what's brave, what's noble,
> Let's do it after the high Roman fashion . . . (IV, xv, 86–7)

However, though her final line has a fine ring to it, 'the briefest end' takes a full act to accomplish, and does not come without her having 'pursued conclusions infinite of easy ways to die', and almost gone over to Caesar. There is still considerable suffering to be lived through before she can claim Antony as her husband. Our response to these sufferings determine finally the effect of the tragedy as well.

5. *The Tragic Effect*

i) *Antony is dead*

Act V of Antony and Cleopatra controls our response to the entire tragedy; it contains the key to the tragic effect of the play. The tragic hero is dead, but the tragic events go on, with interesting effects on the audience's responses to both Antony and Cleopatra. This gives to the drama a form that distinguishes it from all the other tragedies. Shapiro defines the effect in this way:

> . . . the play does not end with Antony's death, and so the audience cannot quite accept Antony's image of himself [at death] because . . . the meaning of Antony's death hinges upon Cleopatra's response to it.[1]

Harrier makes a similar point:

> [Antony's] suicide is an impulsive act which, awaiting its effect on Cleopatra, hangs portentously between the limbo of dotage and the heaven of love. We remain to see whether Cleopatra can and will be worthy of Antony's assertion of the first Act: that the nobleness of life is in the embrace of such a pair . . .[2]

Two lines of approach to the final act are thus indicated. Antony's personal qualities are retrospectively revalued by Cleopatra, and this will force the audience to undertake a similar process. Also, Cleopatra herself rises to her own death, in a way which causes us again to revalue her actions in the rest of the play. The strength she finds here has always been latent in her; the fact that she finds it at last makes us see more clearly how it showed in earlier scenes. The effect of the last act extends backwards over the actions of the whole play, as well as forwards to the death with which it ends.

Several smaller issues are also touched upon in these two scenes, and two of these have puzzled all critics: the scene with Seleucus, which may seem grossly inappropriate so late in the play, and some confusion about Octavius Caesar's intentions for Cleopatra, and Cleopatra's knowledge of these. It will be best if we dispose of these 'problems' first.

[1] Shapiro, *op. cit.*, p. 29   [2] Harrier, *op. cit.*, p. 64

D

Caesar is concerned with Cleopatra only in so far as she might grace his triumph in Rome. Her judgement of his concern for her is fundamentally accurate:

He words me, girls, he words me . . . (V, ii, 190)

Caesar intends to lull her into security, so that she will not kill herself and deprive him of the pleasure of displaying her. His threats against her children (V, ii, 130–2) are a cruder display of power directed towards the same end. Caesar is, in fact, quite open about his aims when speaking to his officers:

. . . her life in Rome
Would be eternal in our triumph . . . (V, i, 65–6)

and his promises of kindness, gentleness, and even freedom are, quite simply, lies. Cleopatra, thus, is quite right in assuming that he intends to humiliate her, and her active imagination (coupled with a vision of imperial Rome that is remarkably like Elizabethan London) fills in the details. Her response to this knowledge should not surprise us; it weighs heavily in her motivation towards death, adding an intensely personal fear to her desire to act by an impersonal code of loyalty. There is here nothing unexpected, nothing to cause us to lose sympathy with her. As far as Caesar is concerned, this deliberate doubleness can only add to the distaste we feel for the victor, and to our sympathy for the defeated.

The difficulty of the Seleucus scene is whether or not it is staged by Cleopatra—in part or as a whole. Professor Brents Stirling advances what seems to me the best explanation of this episode.[3] In his view, Cleopatra has arranged with Seleucus that the accounts shall be dramatically offered to Caesar, hoping thus to win some sympathy from him. To cover herself, she has also arranged to keep back a good deal. Seleucus then really betrays her trust, and she is genuinely furious that her plot has failed. This seems entirely true to character. Cleopatra is still not finally committed to death when she begins the plot, but is developing that strength. Thus, as Stirling argues, her actions from Act IV, Scene xiv, are best interpreted as advances towards the stability of purpose needed for the suicide, accompanied by lapses of purpose, in which the old Cleopatra with that intense desire for life, reasserts herself. These 'opposing qualities cannot be weighed discursively, but must be sensed together'. The confusion of the scene thus reflects a confusion that overtakes Cleopatra'

[3] 'Cleopatra's Scene with Seleucus: Plutarch, Daniel, and Shakespeare' *Shakespeare Quarterly*, Vol. XV, 1964

plot as well as a deeper confusion within herself. Scene ii is a long process of clarifying that confusion sufficiently to enable her to die.

(ii) *A better life*

Through the poetry of Scene ii, we feel that Cleopatra is struggling to find a new quality of strength, while turning back again and again to those other qualities she shows earlier in the play. Act IV ends with her vowing to hold her 'resolution', and it is this capacity to harden herself, control her variousness in order to achieve one specific aim, which appears in two of her important speeches in Act V. The first lines she speaks contain the situation in its full complexity:

> My desolation does begin to make
> A better life: 'tis paltry to be Caesar:
> Not being Fortune, he's but Fortune's knave,
> A minister of her will: and it is great
> To do that thing that ends all other deeds,
> Which shackles accidents, and bolts up change;
> Which sleeps, and never palates more the dung,
> The beggar's nurse, and Caesar's. (V, ii, 1–8)

Cleopatra is here intent upon coalescing into one sharp act of determination the fleeting states of her previous being. But the 'better life' that is impervious to the fluctuations of fortune and change is, ironically, death. Accident, change, mortality can only be 'shackled' and 'bolted' by a voluntary act of death—and that act, as in Antony's case, can have no value for the living. Suicide may suggest that the queen has a capacity to act and assert her freedom from Caesar. To the audience, however, it will also assert her lack of freedom to act otherwise. Cleopatra, established over the whole play as a symbol of life, fertility and 'infinite variety', discovers herself through an act that is a denial of all she symbolises. And yet, in its own context, it is an act that finally fixes our sympathy with her. Our emotional response cannot simply be that it is 'good' that Cleopatra, by taking her life, is at last acting in a responsible, loyal, Roman fashion. Nor, of course, can we feel simply disappointment that she does not put Antony aside, as she has done others, and turn her charms upon Caesar. There *are* values in the attitude that carries her to her death: the ambivalence is that they are not the values by which she has lived.

The same ambivalence is felt in the imagery of her other speech of determination to die:

> My resolution's plac'd, and I have nothing
> Of woman in me: now from head to foot
> I am marble-constant: now the fleeting moon
> No planet is of mine. (V, ii, 237-40)

In one way, we are asked to approve of the constancy of the purpose that she here proclaims. Her repudiation of the 'fleeting moon' is necessary in her new situation. Yet, the speech subtly suggests that this process, as well as strengthening, has also diminished her. 'I have nothing/Of woman in me . . .' must surely suggest a death of fertility, of femininity, which reduces the range of her characteristics, and of our sympathy. Similarly, her view of herself as 'marble-constant' has overtones of a reduction of her humanity to the coldness and hardness of a statue— simply a representation of the real, human thing. We are not at any point allowed to accept her death unreservedly as the ordained end of her struggles. Again, a double vision of the action is provided. We see her vacillations both as weakness, and as a genuine indication that

> she desires more deeply—out of her essential being—to go on with life and power.[4]

(iii) An Emperor Antony

Cleopatra's great speeches on Antony in this scene must also be seen in two lights. First, they are a source of strength to her, showing her that Antony's power quite literally extends beyond the grave, and reaches out to modify her attitudes after his death. Secondly, the words reach out to us as well, providing us with a vision, a dream of 'an Emperor Antony' that makes us see, with renewed clarity, why we should value him so highly. In these lines (76-100) are brought together and raised to a high pitch of intensity all the qualities of life he represents. His power, his friendliness and magnanimity and the scope of his actions are raised to mythic proportions:

> His legs bestrid the ocean, his rear'd arm
> Crested the world: his voice was propertied
> As all the tuned spheres, and that to friends:
> But when he meant to quail, and shake the orb,
> He was as rattling thunder. For his bounty,
> There was no winter in 't: an autumn 'twas
> That grew the more by reaping . . . (V, ii, 82-8)

4 Harrier, op. cit., p. 64

The following image of the dolphin, always troublesome to critics, *suggests* to me the freedom and power of Antony's life, and calls into play age-old associations of the near-divine status of the animal which inhabits, with grace and ease, the elements of air and water. The effect of the image, thus, is to remind us of Antony's attempts to bring two life-styles under his control, to live in two elements at once. The image is typical of the whole speech in that it denies the truth. Antony did not do this; the grace and ease that Cleopatra here attributes to him belong only to the dolphin. Again, we are reminded of the ironic contexts in which the speech is set. It *is* a 'dream', a 'sleep', and we realise that Cleopatra is recreating Antony in her imagination, not as he was, but as he might have been. Once again, the 'lyric imagination' makes its gesture against the 'brute fact', and yet there is sufficient truth in her version for it to give her aid at this moment. *We* are forced to see that Antony's nobility as a character lies not only in his acts, but also in his capacity to evoke this response in another person—as we have already seen happen in the case of Enobarbus. This power of one personality to act on another through gestures (for Cleopatra's speech is really a long list of Antony's dramatic gestures) means that, for the audience, a final judgement on a character cannot be reached even with his death. Antony is still a determining force in Cleopatra's every living moment. She creates her own belief in a figure of her own imagination, and, holding to this, gains the strength to face death.

Yet even this process is undercut by ambivalences. The most immediate of these is that she only realises Antony's worth after his death. Again, the action substantiates Antony's early judgement that

> . . . love is never link'd to the deserver
> Till his deserts are past . . . (I, ii, 184–5)

a judgement which, as we have seen, he has been unable to apply to himself. If Cleopatra's speech here shows a moving awareness of Antony's merits, it reminds us forcibly of her unawareness of the same merits while he lived.

(iv) *All length is torture*

A long movement of indecision and confusion intervenes between these speeches of memory and commitment, and her actual death. Caesar's calculated lying is given full scope to defeat itself—which it must for the audience that already has Dolabella's word that Caesar intends to lead Cleopatra in triumph (line 110), and has heard Cleopatra's own previous commitment to death (line 70). The Seleucus episode gives us, however, a sense that Cleopatra is being led slowly away from her commitment, and when a countryman enters, carrying a basket of figs, the scene, and her purpose, might appear to have lost all direction. However, Shakespeare has already contrived to suggest that Cleopatra has some plan to outwit Caesar (she whispers instructions to Charmian in lines 191–4), and her first words to the Clown make clear his role in the plot:

> Hast thou the pretty worm of Nilus there
> That kills and pains not? . . . (V, ii, 242–3)

The bitter humour of the brief interlude that follows is quite in keeping with the tone of this tragedy. We have seen, in Act IV, a kind of desperate gaiety in Antony's facing death, and the jesting about the 'worm' (with the possible sexual innuendoes) creates a comparable atmosphere around Cleopatra's death. The Clown's errors of expression and meaning give poignance to the approaching tragedy, especially as Cleopatra is allowed to pick up and echo his phrases. For instance, the Clown says of the asp that

> his biting is immortal (lines 245–6)

and moments later Cleopatra tells her women:

> . . . I have
> Immortal longings in me . . . (lines 279–80)

In both cases, the poignancy of the approaching death is suggested by the implied contrast of 'immortality' with the 'mortal' act intended. The 'worm' is the agent of death, and as such plays his part in the ritual of the scene. Cleopatra, in one of her manifestations, is herself the 'serpent of old Nile', the asp, and is thus, as it were, returning once again into that out of which she grew. This impression is reinforced by frequent images, earlier in the play, of the Nile as the source of life, and by Cleopatra's own reference to this life-giving mud earlier in this scene:

> . . . rather on Nilus' mud
> Lay me stark-nak'd, and let the water-flies
> Blow me into abhorring . . . (V, ii, 58–60)

Thus, again with characteristic ambivalence, the sources of life and death are rooted in the same images, and, in placing the asp ceremoniously on her breast, Cleopatra dies by her own hand.

The Clown's remarks also serve to underline the futile aspect of her death.

> For indeed, there is no goodness in the worm

he remarks (265–6), and 'indeed' only death can be expected from the snake. For Cleopatra, there is no 'goodness' in that.

(v) *This great solemnity*

The emotional effect of the death scene itself is quiet and restrained. The formality of Cleopatra's speeches is echoed in the choric background utterances of Iras and Charmian. They sound, in an antiphonal way, several of Cleopatra's dominant characteristics—'eastern star', 'lass unparallel'd' and 'royal'. The last two comments remind us also of the speeches of Enobarbus, in which he concentrated our attention upon her regality *and* her spontaneity. The ritual quality of the scene is suggested by Cleopatra's own view of it as 'play'; and several critics have commented on the fact that, in dressing herself in her royal robes and arranging even the pose in which she dies, she is reaching out for a role that has grandeur and nobility, to mark her final moments. Cutting through this achieved formality, however, are several perceptions reminiscent of the earlier Cleopatra. Death is seen as the loss of the pleasures of wine (281), and then as

> a lover's pinch/Which hurts and is desired. . . . (294–5)

Finally, 'heaven' is one of Antony's kisses, which Cleopatra is afraid will go to Iras, if she dies first. So, within the royal calm, within the tenderness and dignity of the death, the vitality and irreverence of the old Cleopatra can still be felt. On the stage, the costumes and the grouping of the characters will strongly suggest the tragic stasis, the moment held still for our contemplation before the drama moves on to its conclusion. By this act, Cleopatra has asserted an equality of courage with Antony, and has proved her right to call 'Husband, I come.'

Yet, even this is not the secure tragic conclusion that it at first appears. Shakespeare, having shown the element of futility in Antony's death, through the ironies of situation with which he surrounds it, reminds us, at the end, that the moving spectacle of the Queen's death is also no reconciliation of the 'warring opposites' of the play:

> Come, thou mortal wretch,
> With thy sharp teeth this knot intrinsicate
> Of life at once untie . . . (V, ii, 302–4)

In Cleopatra's 'intrinsicate', we can perhaps perceive two meanings. 'Intricate', obviously; but, perhaps, also 'intrinsic', hinting that life is intrinsically a knot, a tangled, confused combination of strands, difficult to unravel. If we relate this to the visual image of the asp actually biting through this knot, we are left with the strong suggestion that the tragic acts do not completely assert the triumph of the characters over circumstance. The complications and ambivalences of their lives are not resolved or reconciled by the stroke of the sword or the bite of the asp. They are simply terminated.

In this way, this final image catches the characteristic tragic feeling of the play. To put things right, to set the time in joint again, are not tasks laid before Antony and Cleopatra. Even Caesar's triumph is nothing more than a personal victory over a man who threatened his position; it is not part of some re-assertion of an order to which Antony was hostile. In the play, neither the Roman values nor the Egyptian triumph. We see 'duty' fail to hold Antony, and we see that 'love' cannot be reconciled with the social and military obligations of the Empire. Consequently, this play does not offer the final satisfaction of a new order that we feel in *Macbeth*, nor our sense of achievement and conclusion as Hamlet, in one act, avenges his father and purges the Danish court. Caesar, the character we respect least, speaks the last words, over the dead bodies of those we respect most. In this, *Antony and Cleopatra* differs markedly from the major tragedies. They present a universe in convulsion: the dramatic conflict between the characters is extended by symbolic action and by imagery, to suggest the involvement of the whole of the natural order. *Antony and Cleopatra* presents us more with the image of man in conflict with the fluctuating, but unalterable, realities of *this* world. Antony, we feel, acts *as* he does because the world is as it is; and, as it is, it presents a continual challenge to him. In response to this challenge, he (and Cleopatra) make choices and decisions by which they hope to free themselves from the limitations the hostile world has set around them:

> Lord of lords,
> . . . com'st thou smiling from
> The world's great snare uncaught? (IV, viii, 17–19)

What actually follows from each of these decisions is a gradual narrowing of their lives into a pattern of cause and effect that leads to their destruction. The 'terror' of this tragedy arises from our awareness of the distance between Antony's sense of his freedom, and the inevitable and determining forces that we see closing in on him. Our 'pity', especially strong in Antony's case, arises from our sense of the unfulfilled potential of his life.[5] Once again, we view the fates of the characters in a double light, with the consequent ambivalent response.

In ways which I have tried to suggest in the preceding pages, the play finally achieves a supreme balance, seeing all, judging all in turn, but presenting an unresolved ambivalence. It celebrates life, vitality, sensuality, generosity and variousness—all that elevates the glorious Antony and the vital Cleopatra above Caesar, the cold, political animal. Yet, it shows with equal force that in an unfriendly world, such love, vitality and openness lead only to destruction. It is a play profoundly moving in the evocation and defence of love and vitality; and profoundly pessimistic as to the ultimate fate of both. To the reader, and the audience, it presents the challenge of responding to both attitudes to life as part of the same experience. It is in this that the value of the experience of the play lies for us.

[5] For a fuller discussion of this aspect of tragedy, see Northrop Frye, *Anatomy of Criticism*, pp. 210 ff.

6. Note on the Sources of the Play

The story of Antony and Cleopatra was legendary even in Roman times, passed down the centuries gathering increasing moral undertones, and was probably best known to Shakespeare's audience as a romantic, but cautionary, tale concerning the wiles of beautiful women, and the weakness of the flesh. With the significant exception of Plutarch, the Roman historians took a decidedly hostile attitude to Cleopatra, seeing her as a foreign temptress who seduced and destroyed a great Roman leader, thereby also endangering the stability of the Empire. The two lovers then gained, in literature and in common estimation, the status almost of 'examples' of the destructive power of sensual passion. However, as Bullough shows,[1] the sixteenth century saw a growing sympathy with them, and especially with Cleopatra. This movement may be said to culminate in Shakespeare's treatment of her. By the time of Dryden's *All for Love* (1678), the moralising aspect of the story has re-asserted itself again.

Apart from the very general currency of the story, Shakespeare might have been aware of two other dramatic treatments of the subject. In 1578 Robert Granier published *Marc Antoine*, in which Antony is pictured as destroyed by an erring passion. In 1590, this play was translated into English by Mary Sidney, Countess of Pembroke, and was almost certainly available to Shakespeare. So also was Daniel's *Cleopatra*, first published in 1594. Bullough lists several verbal similarities between both these plays and Shakespeare's. Daniel's play, however, takes a much more moralising attitude to the lovers. The effect of both these earlier works on Shakespeare is apparently almost coincidental; odd snatches of phrasing, individual words and sometimes images come into his mind from his knowledge of the other works. But no hint can be gained that he seriously studied or used either Daniel or Granier.

The case of North's translation of Plutarch's *Lives of the Noble Grecians and Romans* (1579) is quite different. Here, the likenesses are so close that we can almost imagine Shakespeare writing his play with North open next to him. We can classify the major similarities under three headings:

(i) Shakespeare's use of Plutarch's structure of events, and any changes he makes in that sequence. Generally, Shakespeare sticks very closely to

[1] *Narrative and Dramatic Sources of Shakespeare*, Vol. 5, London, 1964

Plutarch, varying it in only two significant cases. He eliminates the fact that, as the play opens, Antony is leaving Egypt, not for Rome, but in order to join the campaign against the Parthians. Antony had, in fact, already reached Phoenicia before receiving news of Fulvia's death (Arden edition, p. 250). It is obvious that Shakespeare gains greater dramatic intensity and character contrast by setting this scene in Egypt.

Secondly, Shakespeare handles the Octavia episode much more symbolically than any historian could. Plutarch recounts that, after the marriage, Antony took Octavia to Athens, where she gave birth to his daughter. The disagreement with Caesar only reached a serious level a year later, by which time Octavia was again pregnant. On this occasion, she managed to mediate between the two and bring about a temporary truce. Caesar then turned his attention to defeating Pompey, and Antony took up again the Parthian campaign. Only some time after this did Antony return to Cleopatra (Arden edition, pp. 253–5). Shakespeare eliminates the temporary truce, and Octavia's intercession with Caesar. In this way, he speeds the action, and also keeps Octavia's character within the limits he requires—symbolic of softness, weakness and a futile attempt to reconcile two opposing forces. She is not credited with any personal strength at all, and gains our pity only as the victim of an ill-judged action. She thus contrasts with Cleopatra in the clearest possible way. The fluidity of the action here provides an interesting example of what Una Ellis-Fermor sees as successful plotting in drama:

> It would seem then that the imagination of the audience or reader is thrown forward by the immense impact of such scenes [as the dramatist chooses] upon a track of emotional experience, to come to rest upon the next scene in its curving flight at which it can alight without interference or loss of momentum, there to be similarly received, directed and flung out again upon its track of discovery.[2]

(ii) The way in which passages from North have obviously been used by Shakespeare as the basis of speeches in the play. Examples include Caesar's speech on Antony as a soldier (I, iv, 55–71), Cleopatra's account of the trickery practised upon Antony while he is fishing (II, v, 8–23), Caesar's speech about Antony's allies (III, vi, 65–76), and, most importantly, Enobarbus's speech describing Cleopatra on the river Cydnus. This last instance gives us an illuminating insight into the way Shakespeare worked. Comparing Enobarbus' speech with North's third person description, we see first the greater concentration and vitality

[2] 'The Nature of Plot in Drama', *Essays and Studies*, 1960

of the poetry. (All this is not intended to deny that North's prose has merits suited to its purpose.) For instance,

> pretie, faire boyes apparelled as painters doe set forth god Cupide . . .

becomes

> pretty, dimpled boys, like smiling Cupids (II, ii, 202)

a concentration of the general effect, together with the addition of a telling visual detail in place of North's repetitious 'pretie, faire'. There is greater vitality in the poetic rhythm itself (as in 'made their bends adornings'); but Shakespeare also strengthens the effect by his choice of verbs. Thus, the perfume '*hits* the sense' and the 'city *cast*/Her people out . . .'; in both cases, the positive verb contributes to our sense of Cleopatra's power. The description is given further immediacy by Enobarbus's tone, as in 'It beggar'd all description', suggesting his inability to find words. This suiting of the speech to the speaker becomes clearer in lines 219–26, where Shakespeare invents the detail of 'Being barber'd ten times o'er . . .' to remind us of Enobarbus's ironic viewpoint, momentarily submerged in his praise of Cleopatra.

Finally, Shakespeare seizes upon a detail in North, about the boys having 'little fannes in their hands, with which they fanned wind upon her', and turns it into a typical 'paradoxical metaphor':

> . . . whose wind did seem
> To glow the delicate cheeks which they did cool,
> And what they undid did . . . (lines 203–5)

He adds, in similar fashion, an image not in North:

> . . . and made
> The water which they beat to follow faster,
> As amorous of their strokes . . . (lines 196–7)

Together, they contribute to our sense of ambivalent qualities inherent in Cleopatra and in the scene.

(iii) Certain concepts and images taken from Plutarch are embedded deeply in the play. The 'fascinating, capricious Cleopatra' comes in essence from Plutarch's presentation of her, though, naturally, Shakespeare gives it greater dramatic development. However, the sympathy Shakespeare creates for her is an expansion and deepening of Plutarch's attitude, and, as I suggested in Chapter 2, Shakespeare may have conceived of the structure of his play as a series of modifications of hostile attitudes to her. Similarly, the images of fortune and the tide are to be found in Plutarch, but are again given point and penetration by association with a consistent pattern of imagery.

Select Bibliography

1. TEXT
The Arden Edition of *Antony and Cleopatra*, edited by M. R. Ridley, London, 1954

2. CRITICISM
In addition to the books and articles cited in the text, the following are helpful:

Bethel, S. L., *Shakespeare and the Popular Dramatic Heritage*, London, 1948
Caputi, A., *Shakespeare's 'Antony and Cleopatra': Tragedy without Terror*, Shakespearean Quarterly, Vol. XVI, Spring 1965
Daiches, D., *Imagery and Meaning in 'Antony and Cleopatra'*, in *More Literary Essays*, Edinburgh and Chicago, 1968
Danby, J., *Elizabethan and Jacobean Poets*, London, 1964
Eagleton, T., *Shakespeare and Society*, London, 1967
Granville-Barker, H., *Preface to Shakespeare*, Second Series, London, 1946
Holloway, J., *The Story of the Night*, London, 1961
Jones, E., *Scenic Form in Shakespeare*, London, 1971
Kott, J., *Shakespeare Our Contemporary*, London, 1967
Krook, D., *Elements of Tragedy*, New Haven, 1969
Lerner, L. (ed.), *Shakespeare's Tragedies: An Anthology of Modern Criticism*, Harmondsworth, 1964
Lloyd, M., *Antony and the Game of Chance*, Journal of English and Germanic Philology, Vol. XLI, 1962
Mason, H. A. *Shakespeare's, Tragedies of Love*, London, 1970
Russell Brown, J. (ed.), *Antony and Cleopatra*, Macmillan Casebook Series, 1968
Spencer, B. T., *'Antony and Cleopatra' and the Paradoxical Metaphor*, Shakespeare Quarterly, Vol. IX, 1958
Stroup, T. B., *The Structure of 'Antony and Cleopatra'*, Shakespeare Quarterly, Vol. XV, 1964

Select Bibliography

Index